P R I N E A S

Photographs by Adrian Joyner
Interview by Professor Jonathan Harris

Introduction

Having bought a Greek olive grove in a valley called Prineas Linda Cox and Peter Huby commenced work on the building of this remarkable house in 2004.

What follows is an interview by Professor Jonathan Harris with Linda and Peter during 2012.

Jonathan was appointed in 2011 as Professor of Global Art and Design Studies at Winchester School of Art, University of Southampton. He had spent the previous twelve years teaching at the School or Architecture, University of Liverpool. He is the author/editor of sixteen books.

The photographs were taken by Adrian Joyner during 2011-2012.

Can you tell me where is your house?

Linda: The house is in Greece, about twelve kilometres from Kalamata in the Peloponnese and it's about 2 kilometres from the coast, overlooking the Messinian Bay, and behind us are the Taygetos Mountains.

How did you first come across the location? Were you just driving around?

Peter: During 2002-2003, Linda had a year off from her work at the school where she was Head of Performing Arts. We went travelling in Eastern Europe. We were in Romania, Bulgaria, Hungary, those kinds of places. We spent the winter in Cyprus and at the end of the winter we came back to the Greek mainland. When we got to Kalamata the weather was very bad, so we rented a room for six weeks and in those weeks we met some people. We camped actually, when the weather improved, on this piece of land which we now own, but at the time it was owned by two English people, Richard and Lisa.

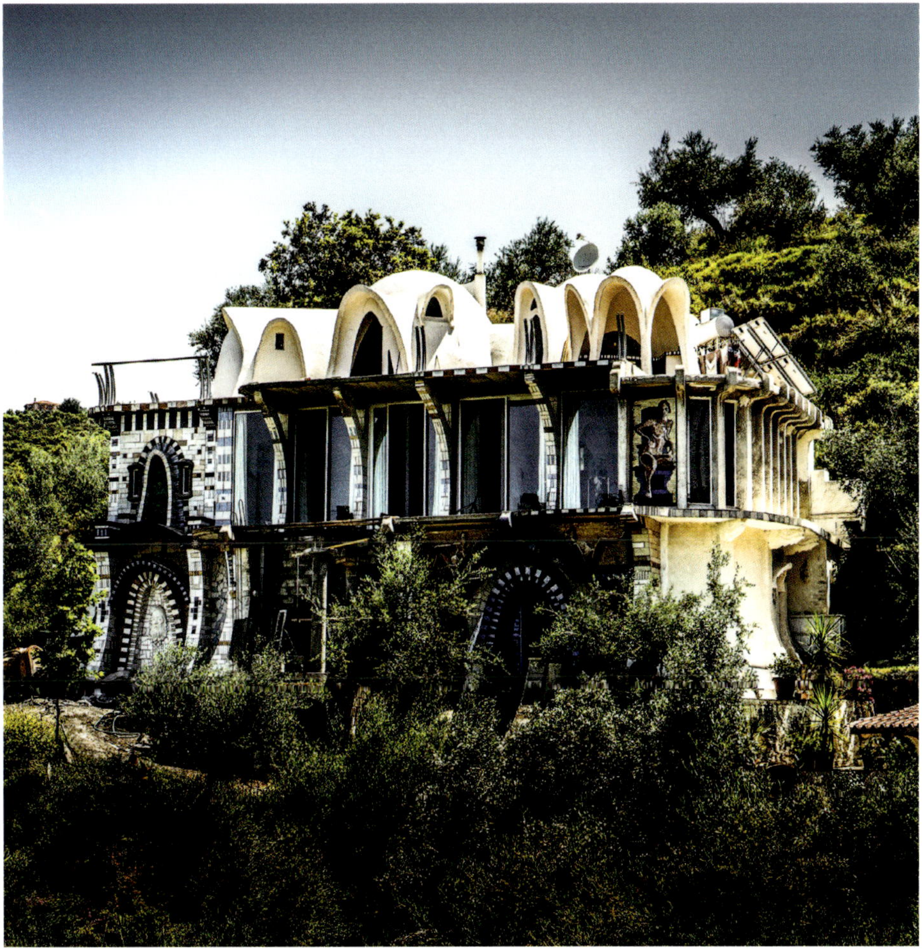

Did you have any sense that it was an obvious site on which to build something?

Linda: No, not really. I guess we were vaguely looking for something though not in any focused way. I thought this land was too steep to build on and that it probably wasn't appropriate for us, and there was another piece of land we were interested in but it was a lot more expensive. In the end, when we bought the land it wasn't necessarily an easy option because it is a very steep site and we've had to do a lot of ground work in order to make it a place where you can put a building.

You do have a view of the sea don't you?

Linda: Yes we do. We have a fabulous view out over the bay and also down the valley. The land we have is one side of a valley so we have a great view of that too.

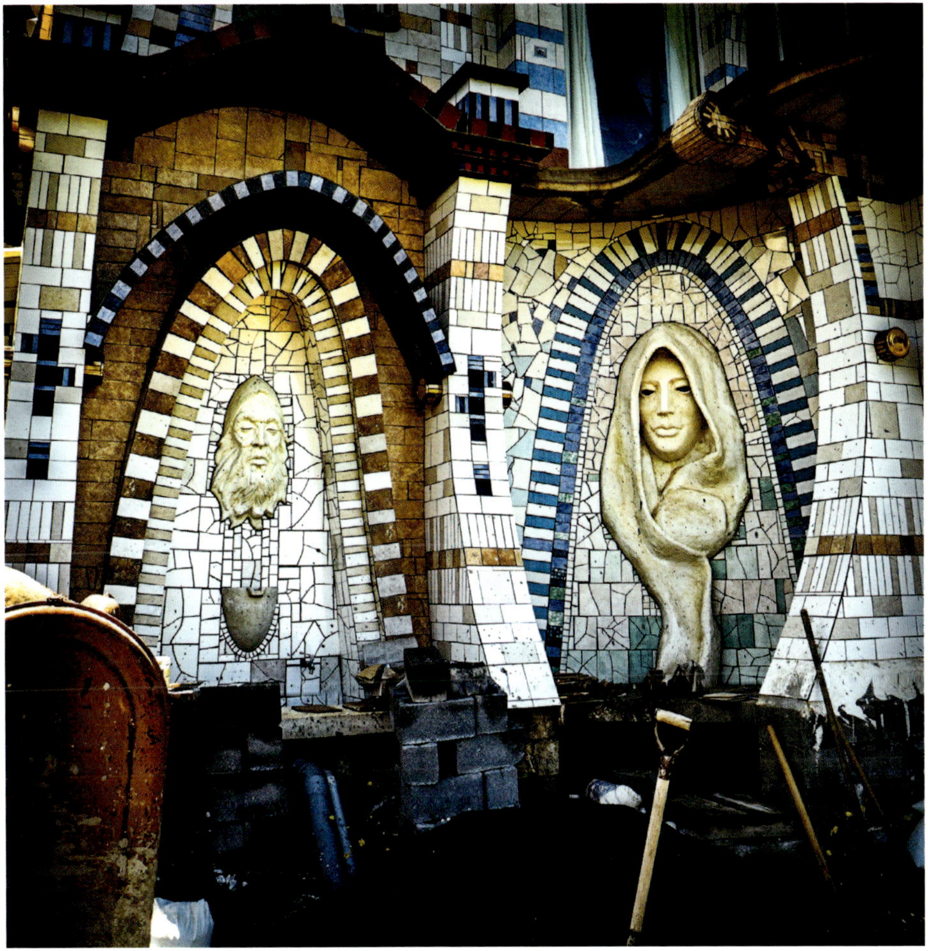

What about neighbours? Did you find that the people living round about seemed sympathetic to the idea of you moving onto the site?

Peter: Yes, given that, at the time we spoke very little Greek. Our immediate neighbour Nikos Avramis has a house in the village and olive trees next to ours. He was just very good to us and he and his family have been very supportive. I worked for him on the first olive harvest to get the hang of things and after that we were able to do our own. We have two hundred olive trees of our own. Because of the shape of the building that we were putting up, some of the locals thought it was going to be a church. It was quite good for us really. They thought we were religious type.

How did you come up with developing an idea for what you might build? Did you have plans, models, and any clear or systematic notion of what you might do?

Linda: No, (laughs) no to all those things. Peter just started the building. As you know already, there's a wooden house on the site and we spent the first year building that, and a workshop. The main building started after about a year, with a fountain, which is now part of the front of the building, and then it evolved from there really. The ideas came from that.

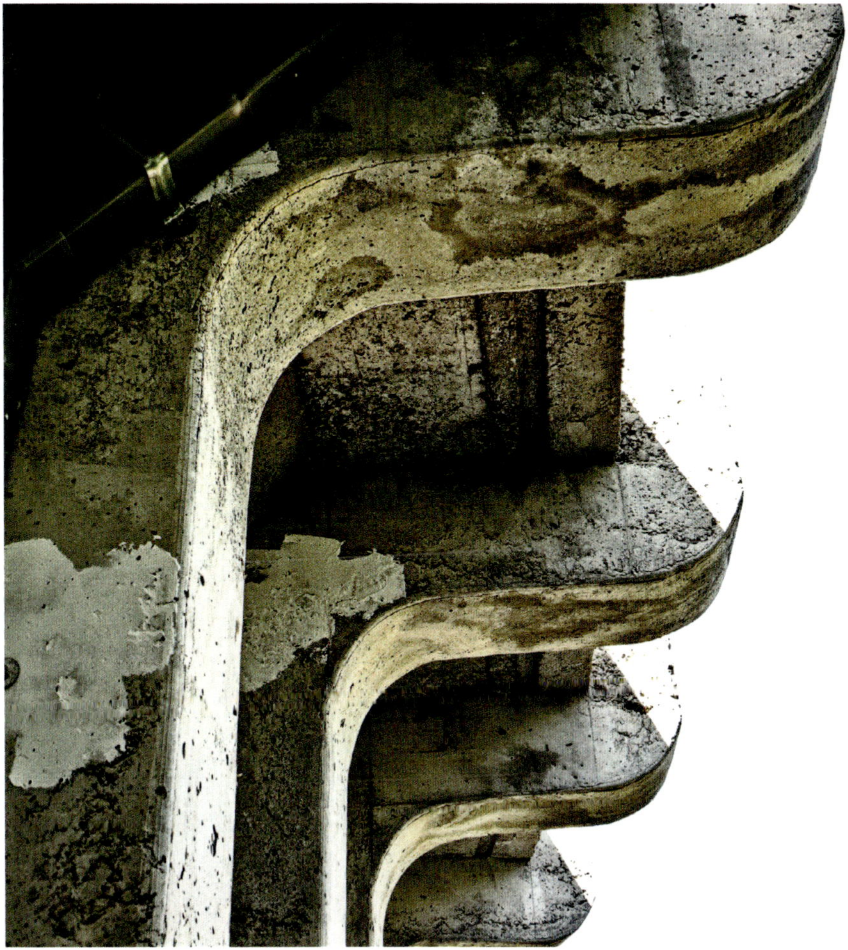

What did you have on paper? Any drawings? Sketches?

Peter: (laughs) No, nothing. It was a 'materials' thing. You have the sand and cement, the blocks, the steel and of course the site itself. Things suggest themselves.

In the UK, I had started a project which used catenary curves and the key to the whole thing is that catenary shape. I guess that if there is a consistent motif, that's what it is.

What about the collection of rooms? Did you have a notion of how many rooms you might have, some sense of how long it might be?

Linda: No, not really. We wanted it to be big enough. We had lived in one big room for a year after we'd been travelling and we liked that sense of space.

Peter: It was an old school.

Linda: And it was great space to be in, so we were keen to have a big space and the rest of it we weren't sure about.

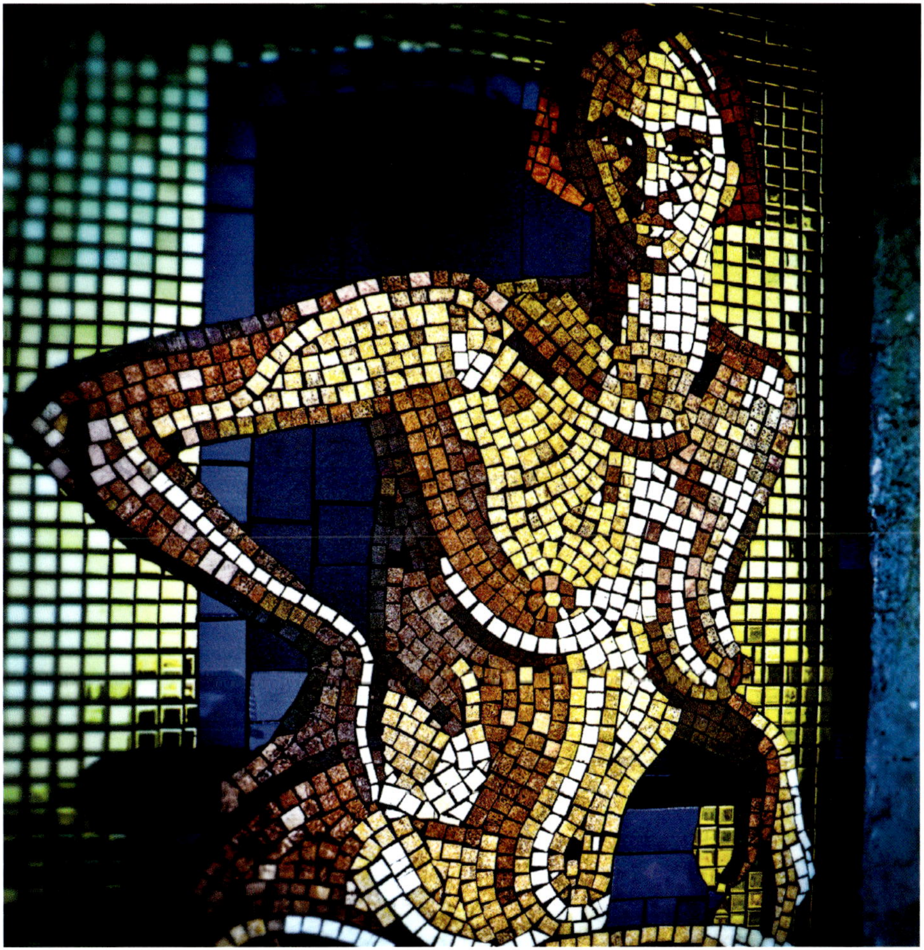

I'm intrigued to know how it was affected by the climate, the temperature in the place. Was that an issue right from the start in terms of trying to get a cool space in the summer?

Peter: Yes, absolutely, and it was good that we had spent the first year building the wooden house because then we had a sense of the annual meteorological cycle, where the sun rose and set at different times of the year. So yes, it absolutely was.

What about winds moving through the property?

Peter: It's very sheltered here. We watch the white caps out in the bay and the wind can be very strong, but the valley is very sheltered, which in the winter is a good thing but in the summer, when you want the breezes, it's not so good. But, just to loop back a bit, one of the things that did affect us wasn't so much the weather but our experience of earthquakes. It's an earthquake area and, I think, once we realised how frequent they were – and we had quite a severe one in the second year we were here – it then began to condition how we thought about the structure.

We began to think a lot more seriously about the stability of it, really. The top storey, and the domes, are very light and strong. Had we not been living in an earthquake zone, things might have gone differently.

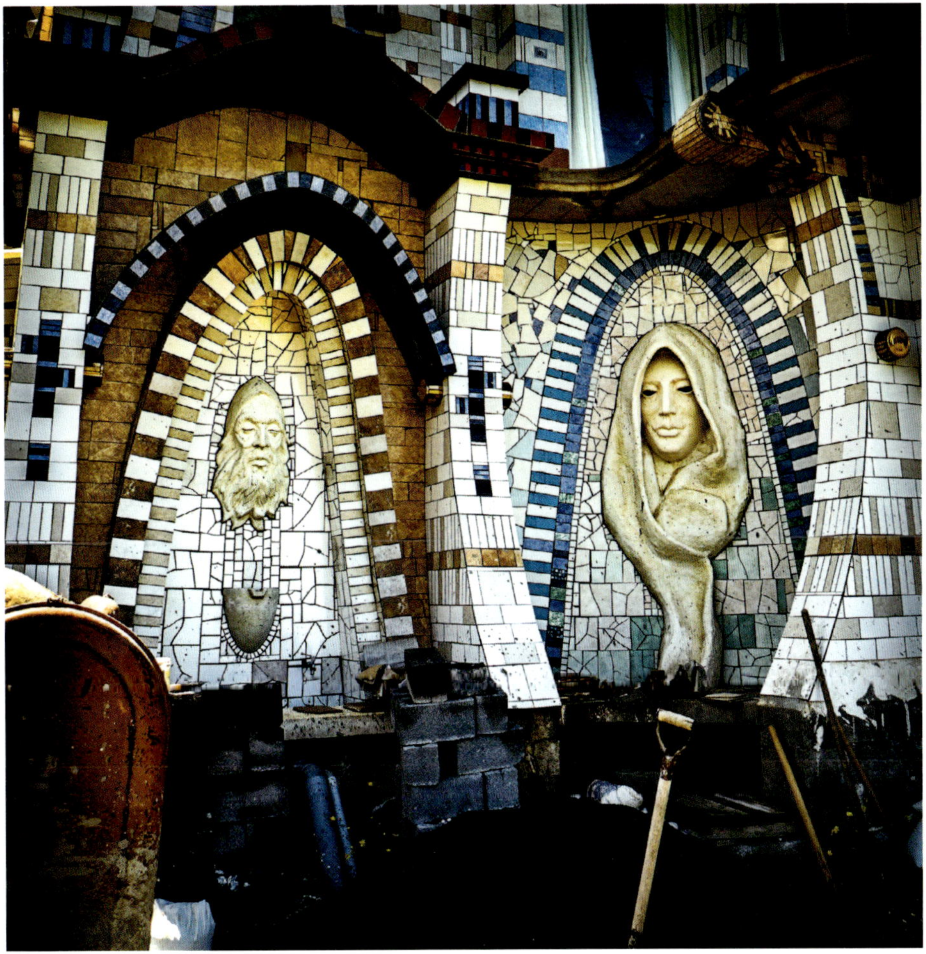

What about health and safety issues generally? Were you confident enough to think you could build a multi-storey building safely? Did you have to do any research into the health and safety aspects?

Linda: Peter is quite observant and I think from the outset, when we first came here, he was very observant of the way that the Greeks do their buildings, the steel reinforcement and how that needs to be tied together, and the amount of steel that they use in the columns. So, from that point of view yes, but no, we didn't do any research as such.

Peter: Were you talking about our safety?

In the house, around the house, yes.

Peter: (laughs) We're very bad. What the house still needs, after seven years, are railings around the balconies. We keep saying, this is the next thing we are going to do, but actually its visitors we worry about. We'll do it, soon.

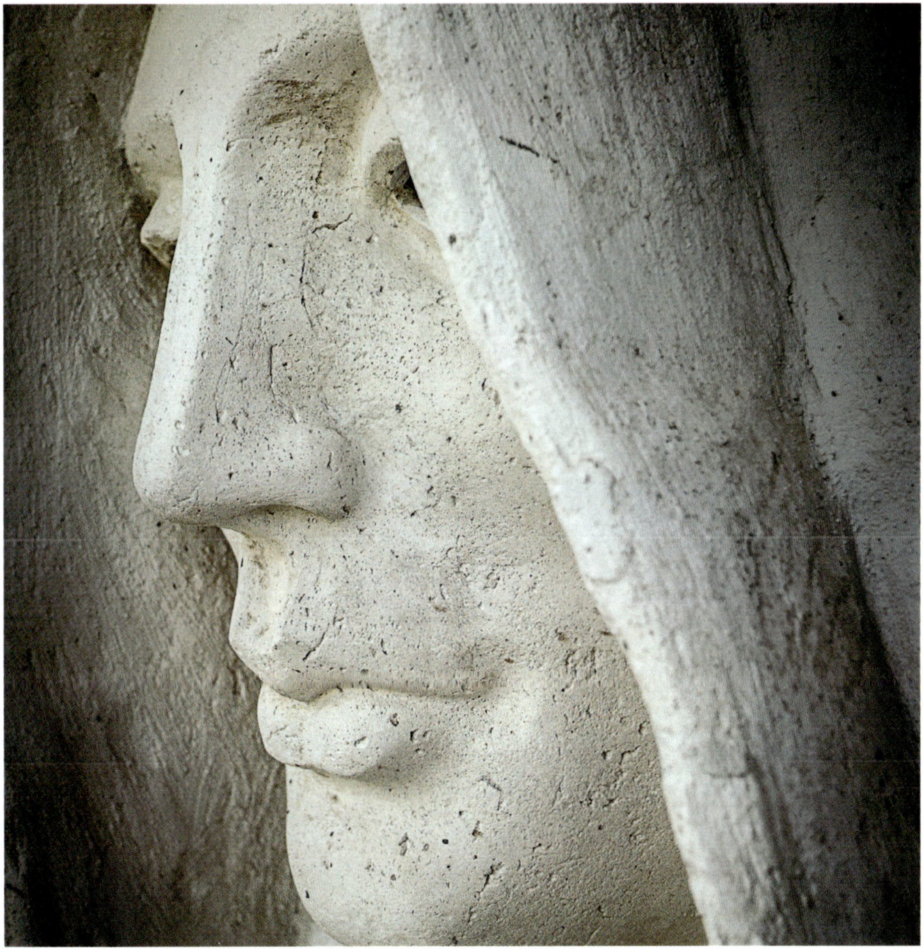

O.K. You decided you would build this house. You were living in the other one. Can you talk about the process of starting to build the new house and your living arrangements at the time? You were living in the wooden house?

Linda: Yes. Prior to the wooden house we were in a tent. We were like the three little pigs. We started off in a tent and then Peter built the wooden house, mostly around us, to get us out of the weather. The whole point of that (the wooden house) was so that he could take his time over the new one and think it through, and not be in a hurry to get us out of the weather.

So, when was this? How long did the process take?

Peter: We've been here eight years. The first year we spent building the wooden house and the workshop, and then we started this almost exactly seven years ago – the big structure. A good biblical number, seven.

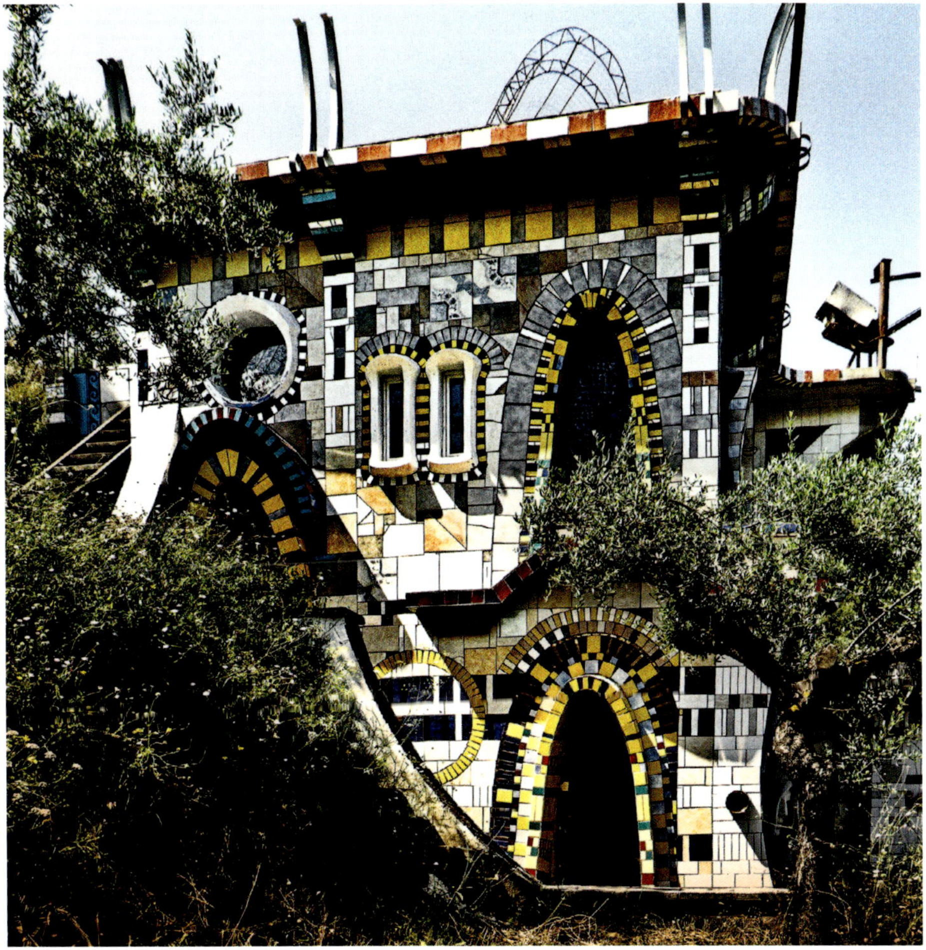

How easy was it to start to get materials to the site, because obviously that road going down to the coast is very narrow and rough?

Peter: Well, when we began… I don't know whether you remember the truck, a one ton open backed vehicle. To begin with, everything came on that truck: sand, cement, everything, and it was really quite hard work because you had to shovel off the sand and gravel by hand, manhandle the cement bags individually. But then I found a builders' merchant in a nearby village who had a very narrow truck, a two ton tipper truck but it was only 1.5 metres wide, something like that, which was able to negotiate our very steep narrow track, which meant that we could get deliveries of stuff. It actually changed our lives. Our project would have been much harder if we hadn't been able to get deliveries. I know the driver, Thimias Milionis, very well because he comes here a lot.

At what point in the process did this happen? How much work had you done?

Peter: Well, a lot – enough to know that it was going to be very hard, which was why we made enquiries about whether it might be possible to find a builder's merchant with a narrow tipper truck. Stavropigio, the village where the Milionis brothers have their business, is maybe 10 kilometres away, not so far, and fortunately they had this truck. It was a felt need really. Had we not found that, we would probably have had to buy one.

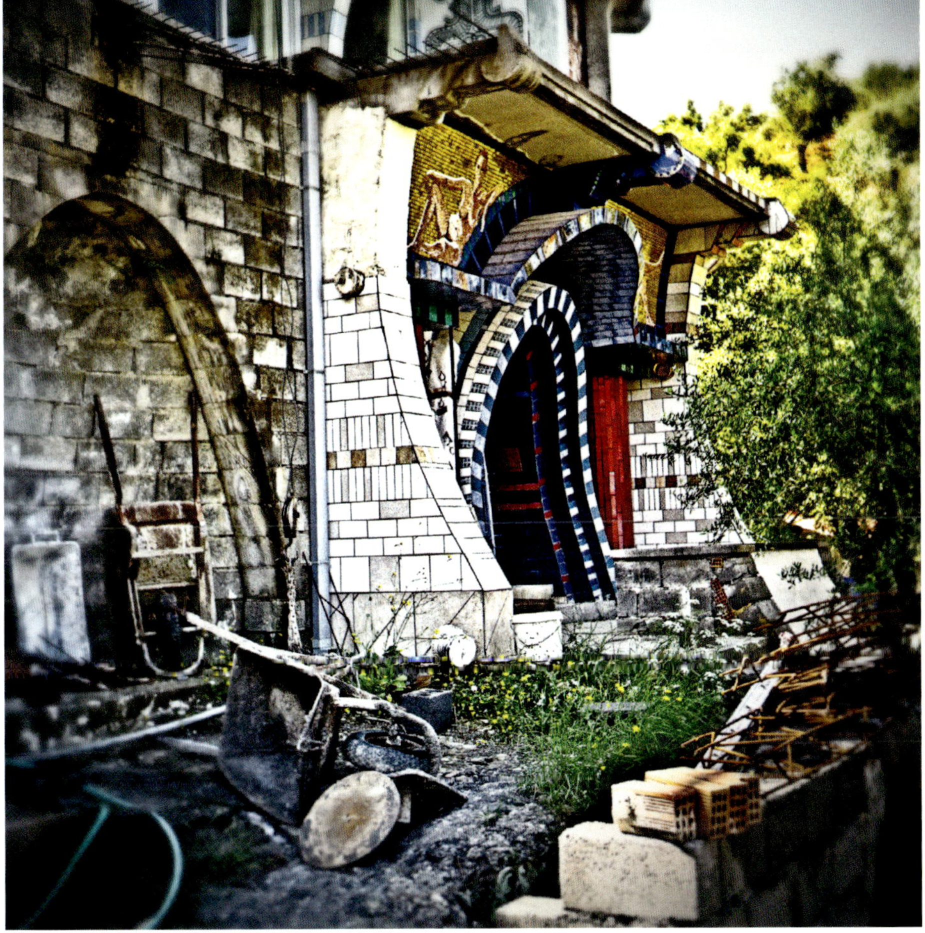

What would your working week be like? Presumably, you had to work to earn money as well as to build the house.

Linda: Well, Peter's living really was building the house. That was his job. He did a little bit of private teaching. I did more teaching. I don't think that at the school they had any idea of the situation we were living in here. I lived a sort of schizophrenic life. Out there I was a teacher doing teaching things, normal things, and here I was a builder really!

So, when you were at work in the school, Peter was there, working away by himself at the house?

Linda: Yes, he would continue.

What sort of jobs, Peter, could you do without Linda's help?

Peter: Almost everything really, but it was just slower, and it's always more companionable to work together. There's no job you can't do on your own, finally, but it's slower, less convenient. You have to do more fetching and carrying.

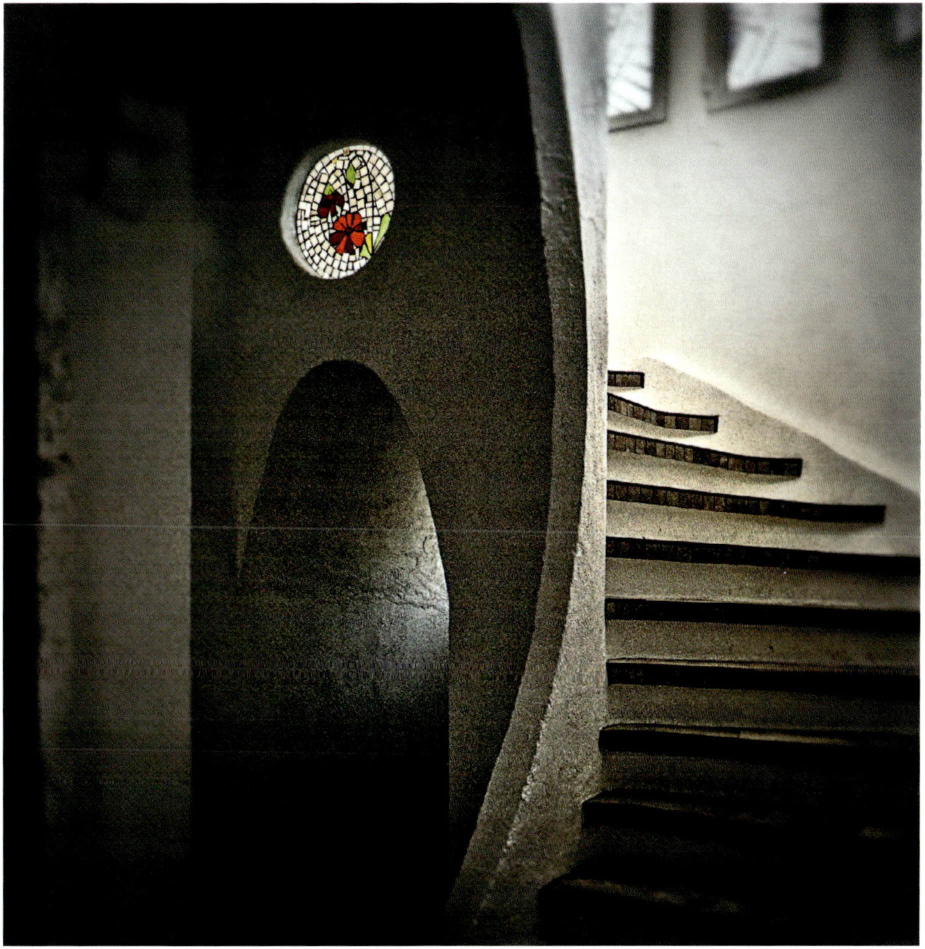

The pleasures of solitary labour, Peter, as opposed to working with Linda, the rhythms of enjoyment?

Peter: I'm a work addict, I think. I could do anything, dig holes. I find there's something redemptive about work.

You like hard solitary labour?

Peter: Well, like is a funny word. I find myself drawn to it.
I'd rather do something than do nothing.

Weren't some of the jobs involving carrying materials or lifting better with two?

Peter: Yes. We had a crane, a geranos, and that was a two person job. You could just about do it on your own, but it was much more convenient with two of us. There were other times when it was much easier with two, and certainly it's pleasanter, more companionable.

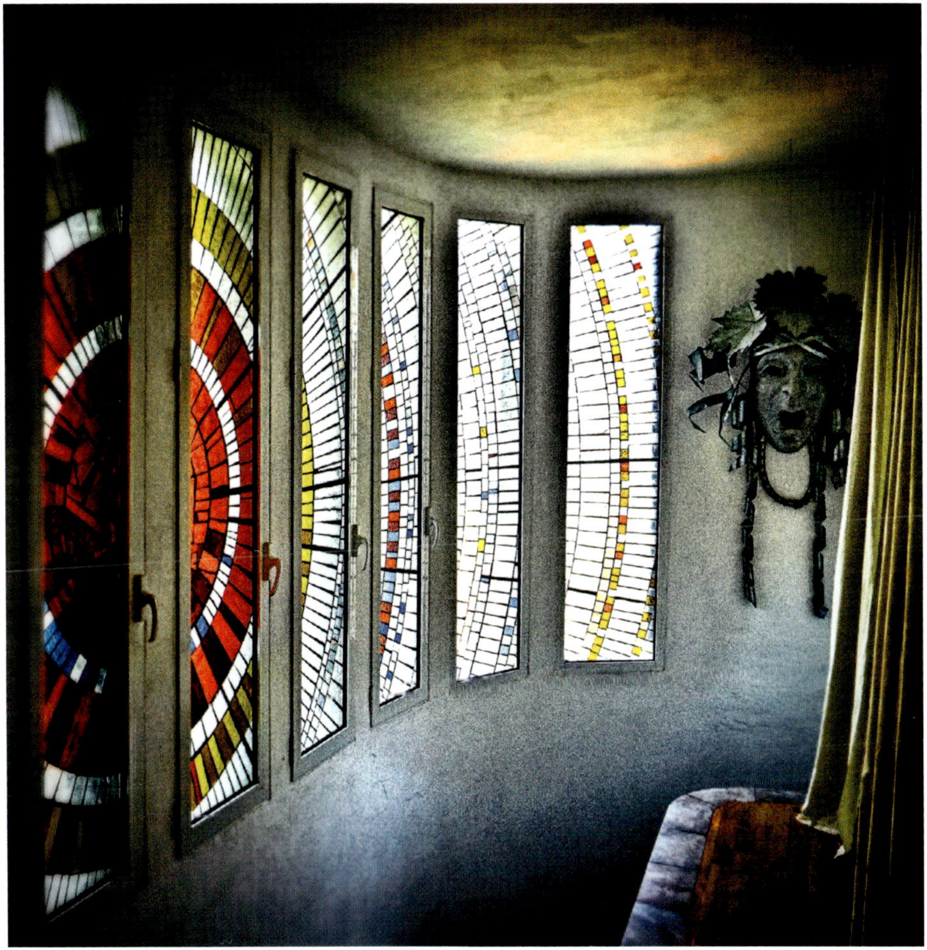

What about expertise? Did you find you had to learn new skills, Peter, or had you already mastered all the necessary ones?

Peter: (laughs) I wouldn't put it quite as strongly as that. Most things yield to common sense. You can watch people who know how to do things and generally speaking, if you're reasonably quick on the uptake, you can learn quite fast. I guess my welding has improved a lot. The technical things, the specifications for the steel and all that kind of stuff was notionally quite difficult but in fact it seems to be applied common sense. I did get hold of a military manual on concrete reinforcement.

I'm sure for you its common sense! It wouldn't be common sense for me … (laughter) … very dangerous. One of the things that interests me here is the range of materials you have to use and the problem of access, and, secondly, the interference, or regulation, by the local state, if any at all. Can we deal with those two questions? What about the substructure of the building, its base? Reinforced concrete, is it?

Peter: Yes, exactly that. We have a cement mixer, so we mixed all our own concrete. As it happens, cement-based materials and steel, though the commodity price of steel does fluctuate, are quite cheap, a good deal cheaper than in the UK. Here, concrete is a natural material. The entire country is made from limestone. Cement is cheap. It's made in Greece, it's not imported.

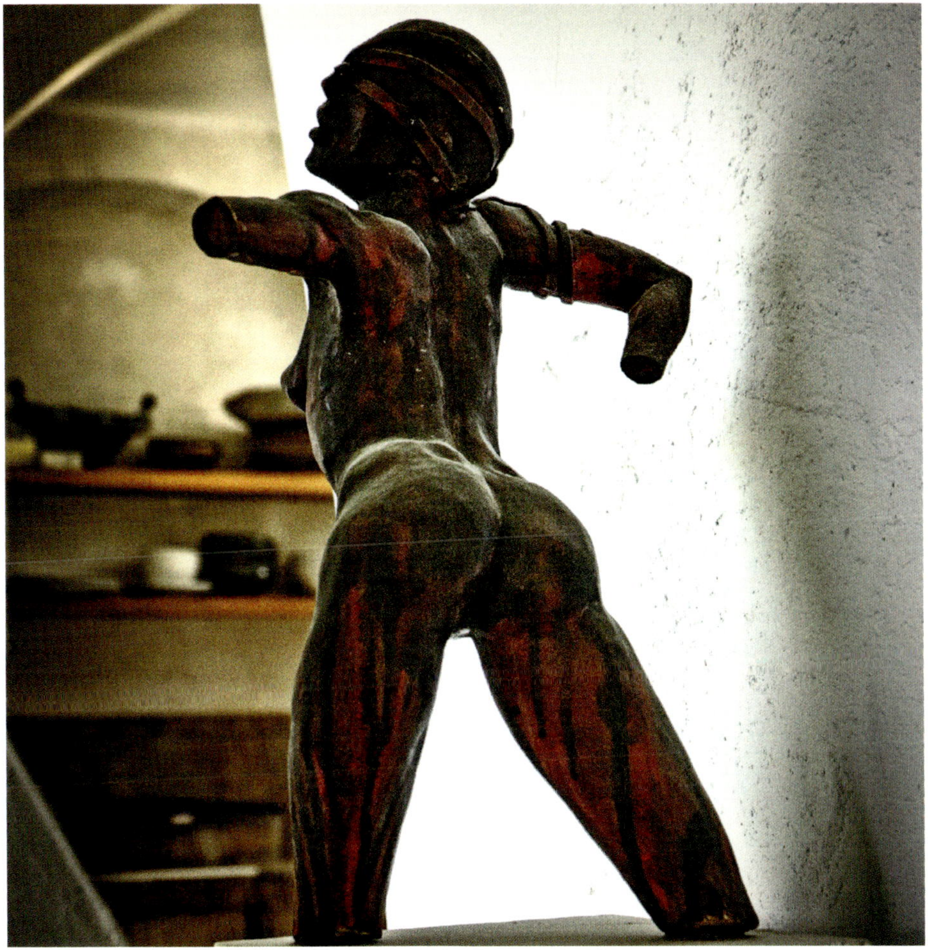

You were already expert in making concrete?

Peter: Well, 'expert,' will remain to be seen, because you never know if you got it right, but my father was a builder, and I worked with him when I was a boy. It's in the bone.

Apart from the concrete, would you say that all the other materials are effectively cladding of one kind or another?

Peter: Yes, mostly ceramic tiles.

Linda: We had a source of free ceramic tiles. We managed to get a lot of free tiles from a factory in Kalamata which was getting rid of all its broken tiles, and because it was a cheap way of covering all the surfaces, that's what we did.

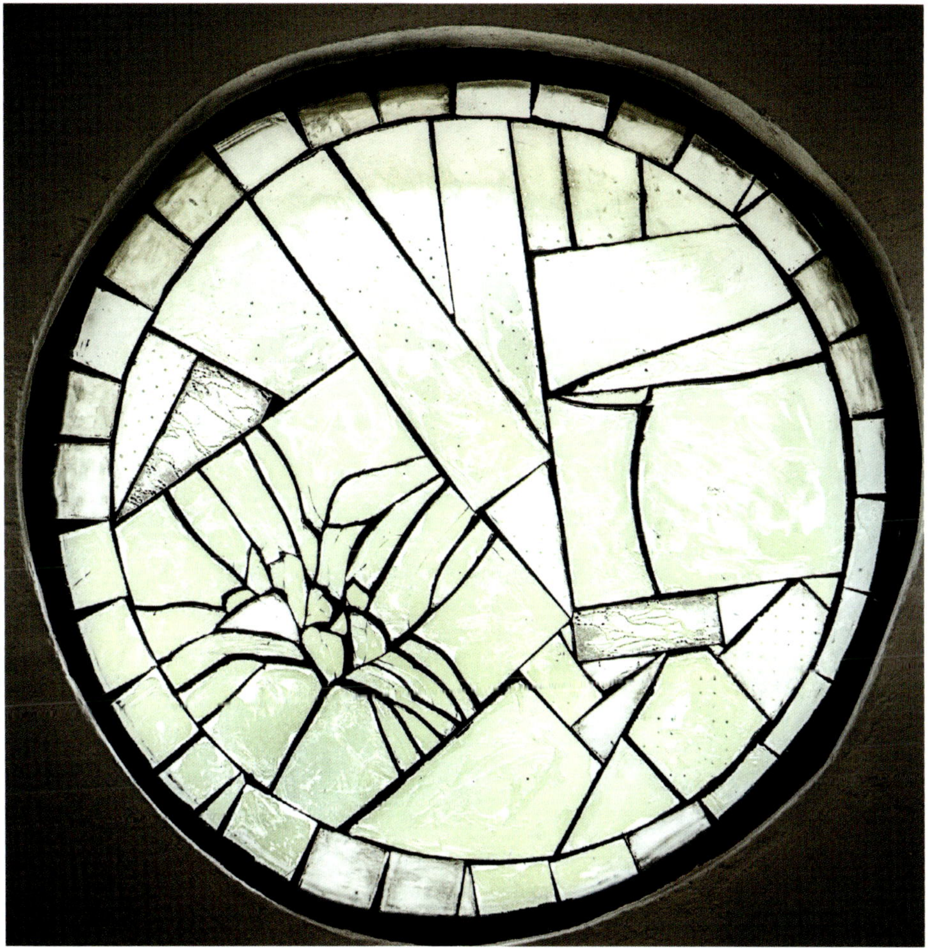

What had these tiles been used for in other situations? What kind of building tiles were they?

Linda: Some of them were wall tiles, some of them were floor tiles. It was a mixture really.

Peter: In a tile works they break a surprising number, in transit, loading and unloading. Stuff gets broken. Corners get broken off. They often have show bathrooms and kitchens, and when these things are dismantled they just trash the tiles.

The outside of the house has some of its arches covered in yellow tiles. There's also a red, almost geometric pattern of tiles, above. What would they have been used for?

Peter: We did have to buy some tiles. When you want a strong colour, like the reds and the yellows, which are, I guess architectural tiles for external use and they're quite expensive, but we tried to keep that to a minimum. Mostly we use stuff that just arrived by happenstance.

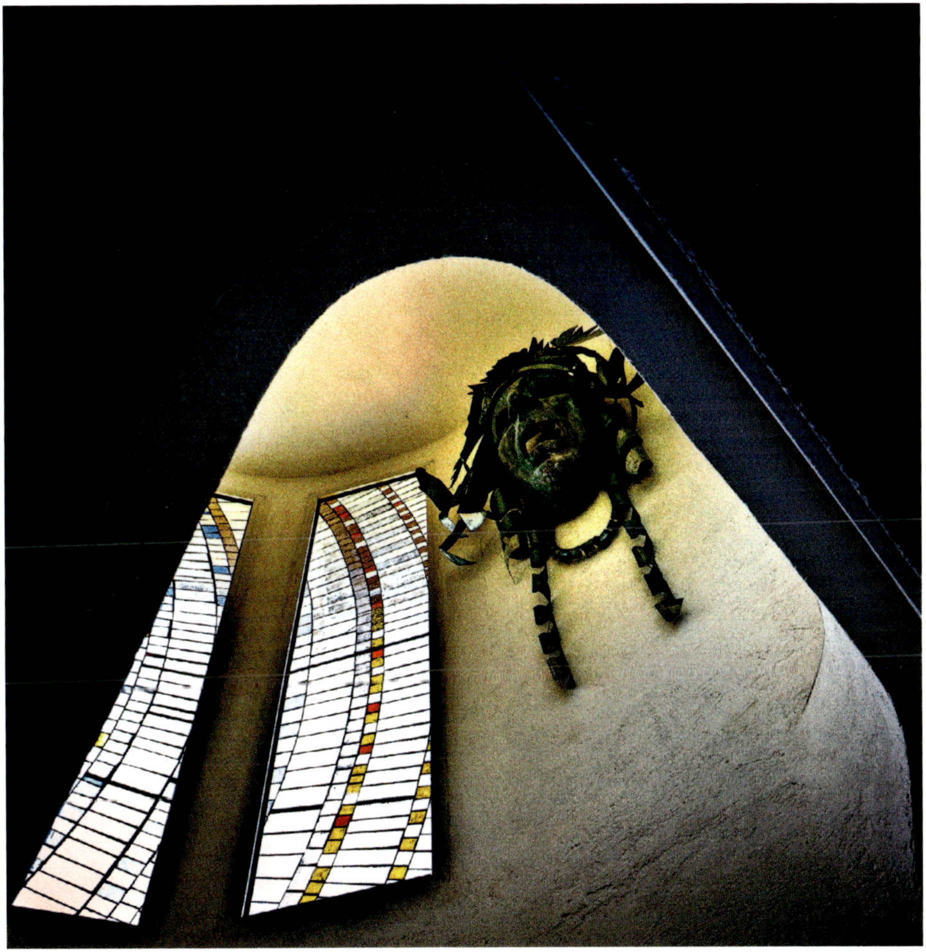

Attached to one of the walls is a big gold disc. What is that made of?

Linda: That was a specialist job. Peter had put those studs through – the actual shape is a cylinder that he'd set into the buttress as he was building. At some point it became clear that we wanted to cover those studs with gold.

Peter: I think in my head they were always going to be gold.

Linda: John Calver is a potter in the UK, a friend of ours, a well known potter I think, and he did those gold discs for us to cover the ends and he also made the gold mosaic around them.

Peter: He came to visit with Viv his wife. They liked the project and it was his gift to the house really.

The cladding has a functional purpose but it's also decorative. It's functional in the sense that it's protecting the house. Is it adding a bit of warmth? What is the value of the tiles in terms of function?

Linda: Well, as you say, it is decoration primarily. In the first instance it was done as a decorative surface but the more we got into it, the more we became aware of the practical benefits. It's extra covering, extra waterproofing, so it does have a purpose as well.

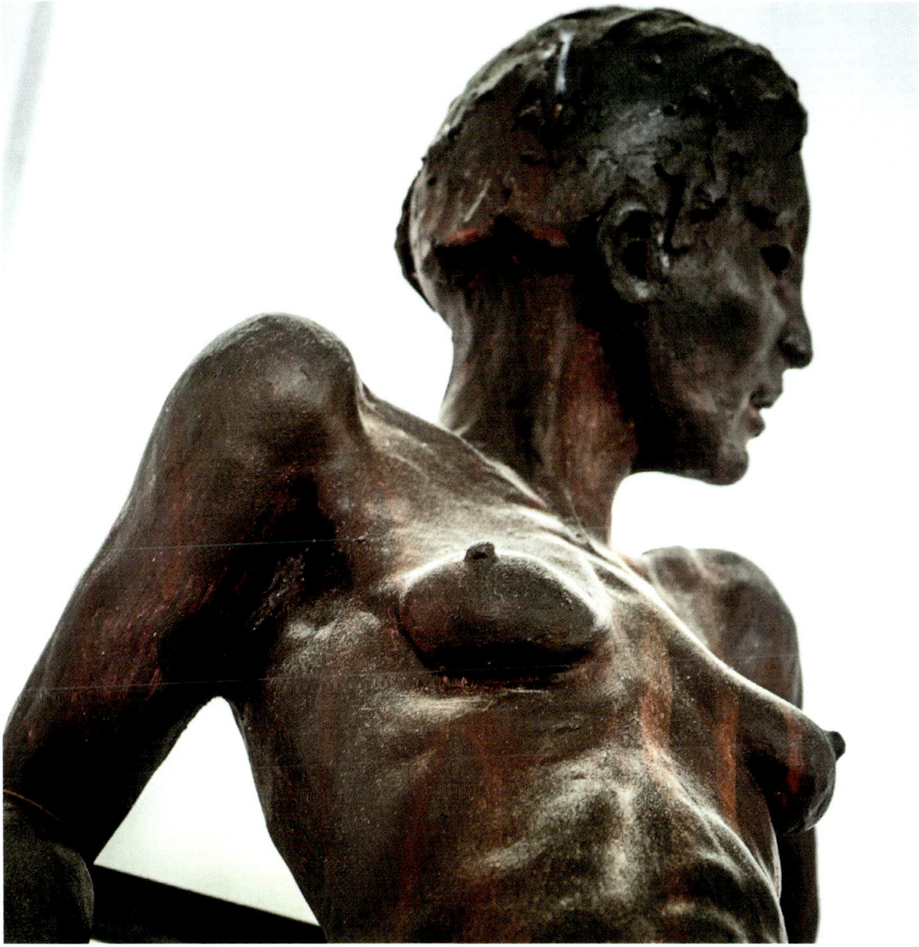

Is it cold in your house?

Peter: There's a mass of material in the house so it does respond quite slowly to heating, and the volume of internal space is very big. So, it's quite ponderous, like a big ship. It warms up very slowly, so it's a good house in the summer. It stays cool but similarly, in the winter, it's quite slow to heat up, the big room anyway.

What about glass? There are a lot of windows. What sort of glass have you got?

Peter: The big square windows are double glazed. The coloured glass is a sort of sandwich of plate glass and coloured glass applied to it, a double thickness of glass.

The big round window is stained glass with red and yellow. How did you make that?

Linda: That's basically the same technique as all the other mosaic. A sheet of clear glass is cut to fit the window frame and pieces of coloured glass applied with silicone to the inside surface.

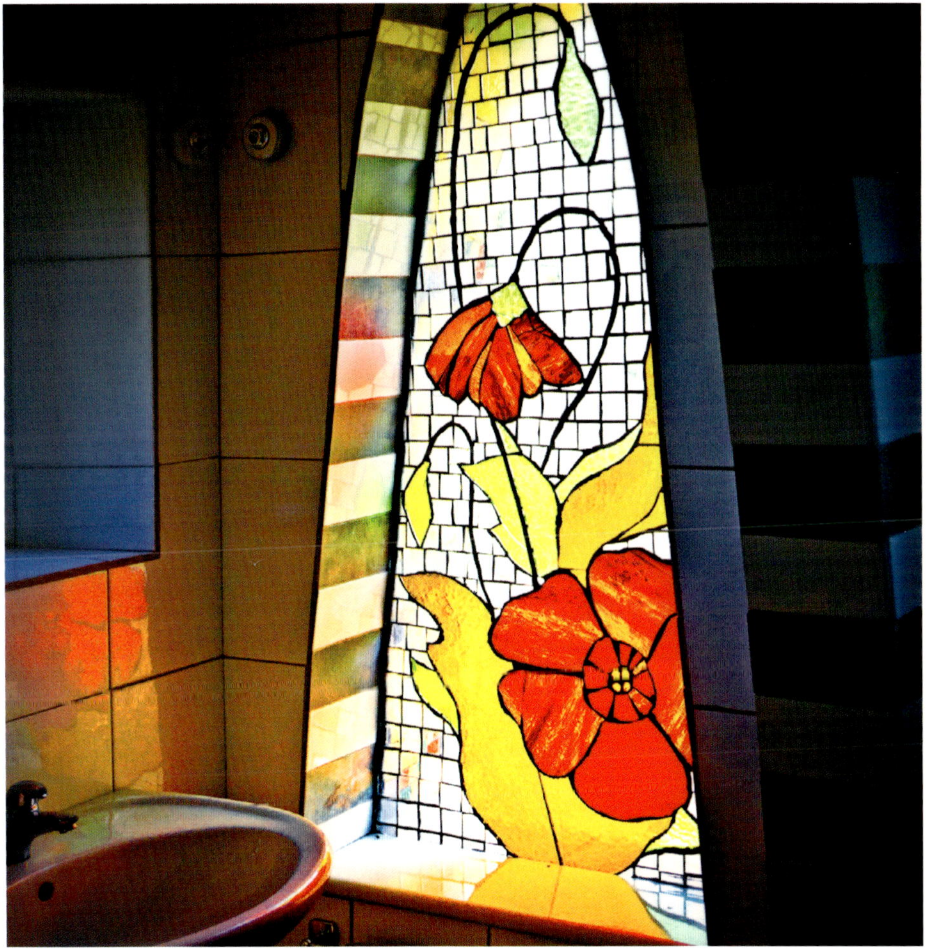

Will it not fall apart?

Linda: The silicone is very good. We grout between the pieces of coloured glass with black grout and a little PVA. It looks like traditional leaded glass and lots of people assume it's a leaded window, but it isn't. Basically it's glass mosaic.

It looks like a big clock face from the inside, 'Big Ben' in London, or something?!

Linda: Actually you can't be miserable in this living room because the window's very brightly coloured. We've kept everything else inside plain because it's such a big feature, and when the sun comes round in the afternoon it shines like a big lantern.

So the sun comes round from the land?

Linda: Behind us, from the mountains behind us. It passes round the back of the house and the side that has the big coloured window.

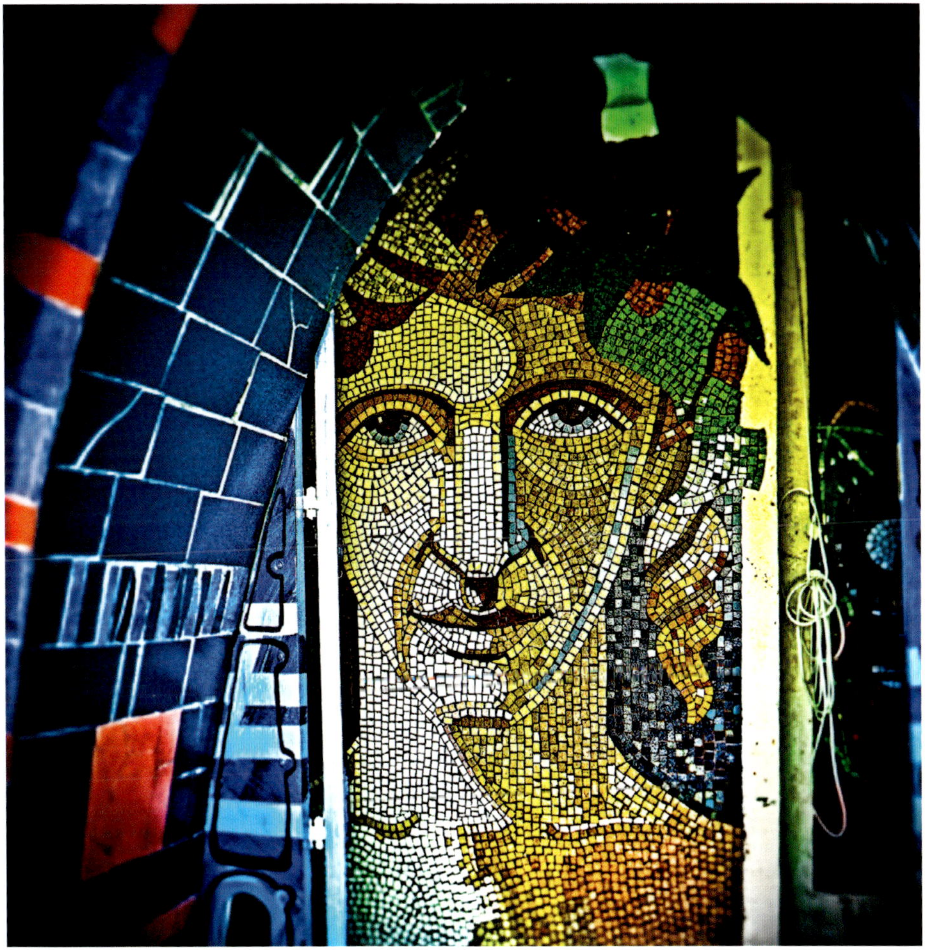

In the middle of the day, in summer, where is the sun in relation to the house?

Linda: In the summer it's much higher in the sky but the general passage of the sun is across the back of the building. The balcony on the front is quite a shaded area.

Do you find yourself in certain rooms to avoid the heat in the summer? Do you migrate to certain parts of the building that are cooler?

Linda: We close the curtains. Most of the buildings here have big retractable awnings to keep the sun off. We've not been able to put one up yet because we haven't got a railing to fix it to, but we will have awnings as well, to keep the sun off the big balcony. The heat tends to bounce up off the concrete balcony and into the living room so it can get quite hot in the summertime.

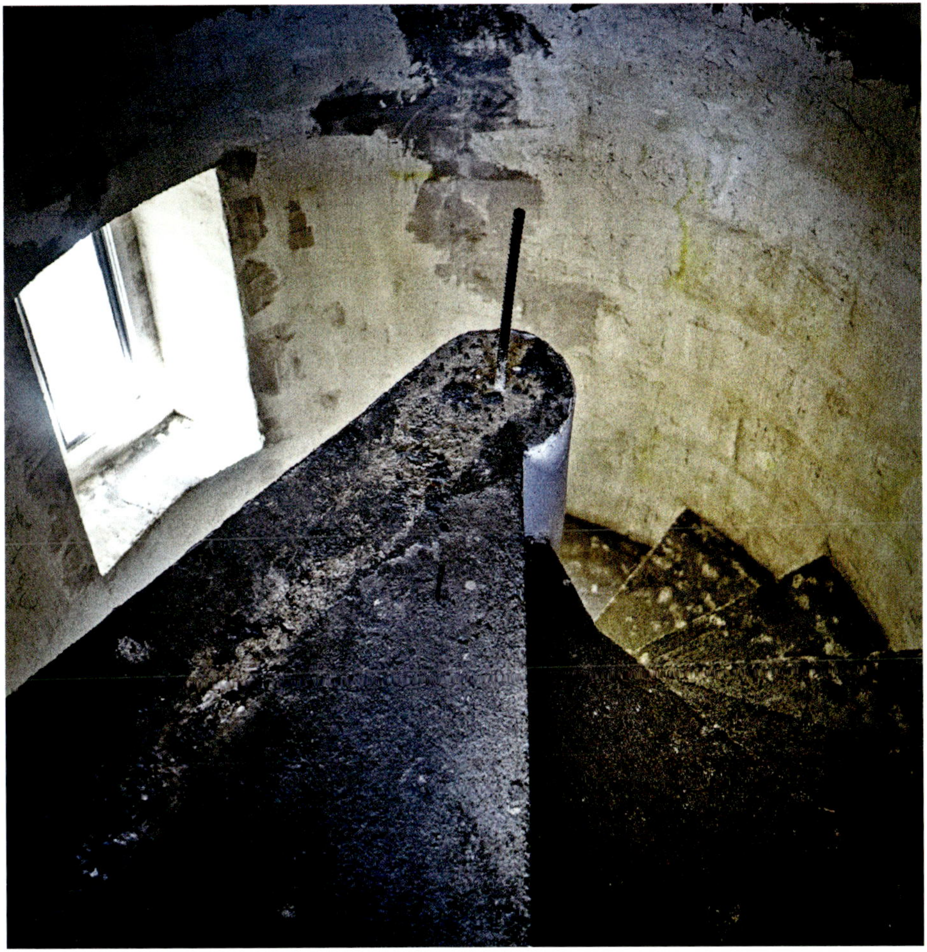

What about the impact of the sun on the materials? Is there any damage to the tiles? Do they not get extremely hot?

Linda: They don't seem to have taken any damage. Frost would have been a bigger problem in that respect, but we don't get frost here. I guess we couldn't do anything like this in the UK because frost would spoil the tiles, split the glaze from the surface. There has been only one occasion in the past eight years when we had icicles hanging from the wooden house. We very rarely get frost.

How long did it take you to build the house? What is your sense of the number of hours or days or weeks or months you spent building it?

Peter: All the visitors who come, particularly the Germans, say, 'Oh, so much work!' Some thousands of hours I guess, tens of thousands, I don't know. I work almost every day.

For how many years?

Peter: Seven.

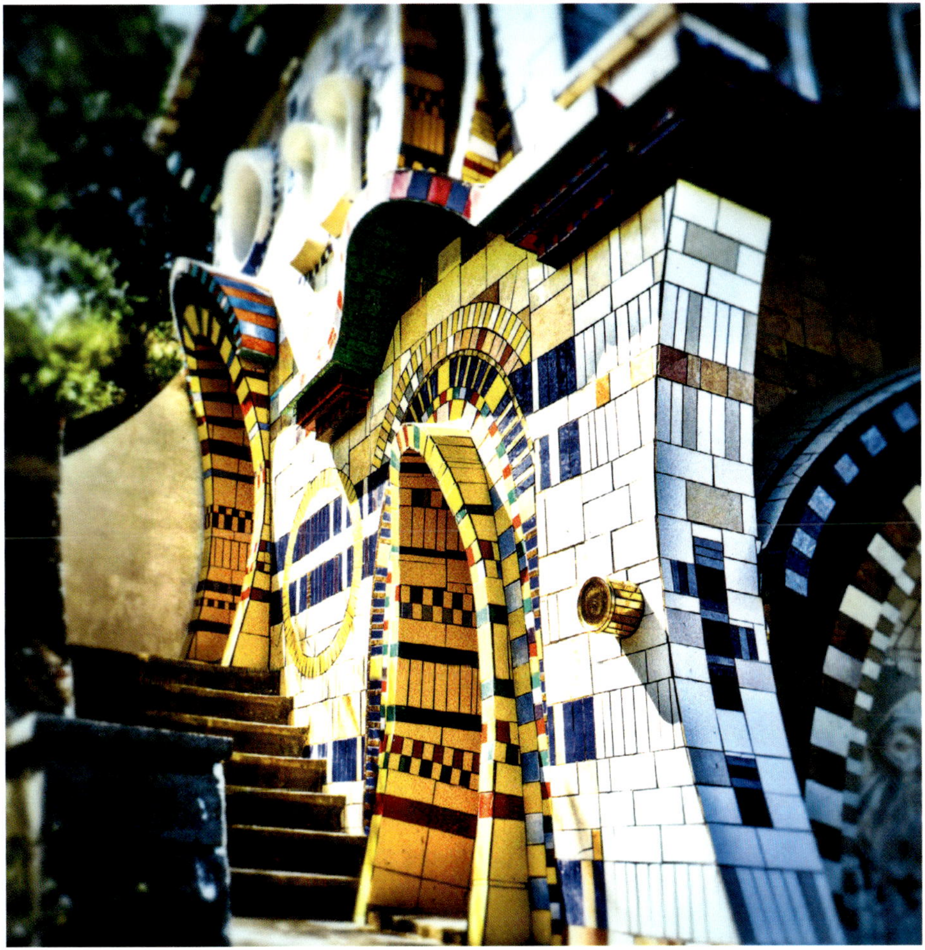

Almost every day for seven years?

Linda: And that's seven days a week.

Peter: Unless we're away. Sometimes you have to take half a day off to go shopping or find building materials. Generally I'm here.

Linda: He does it for pleasure. When the Germans think about the amount of work, they're equating it with working for a living, but for Peter its pleasure. It's what he wants to do. He would do it anyway.

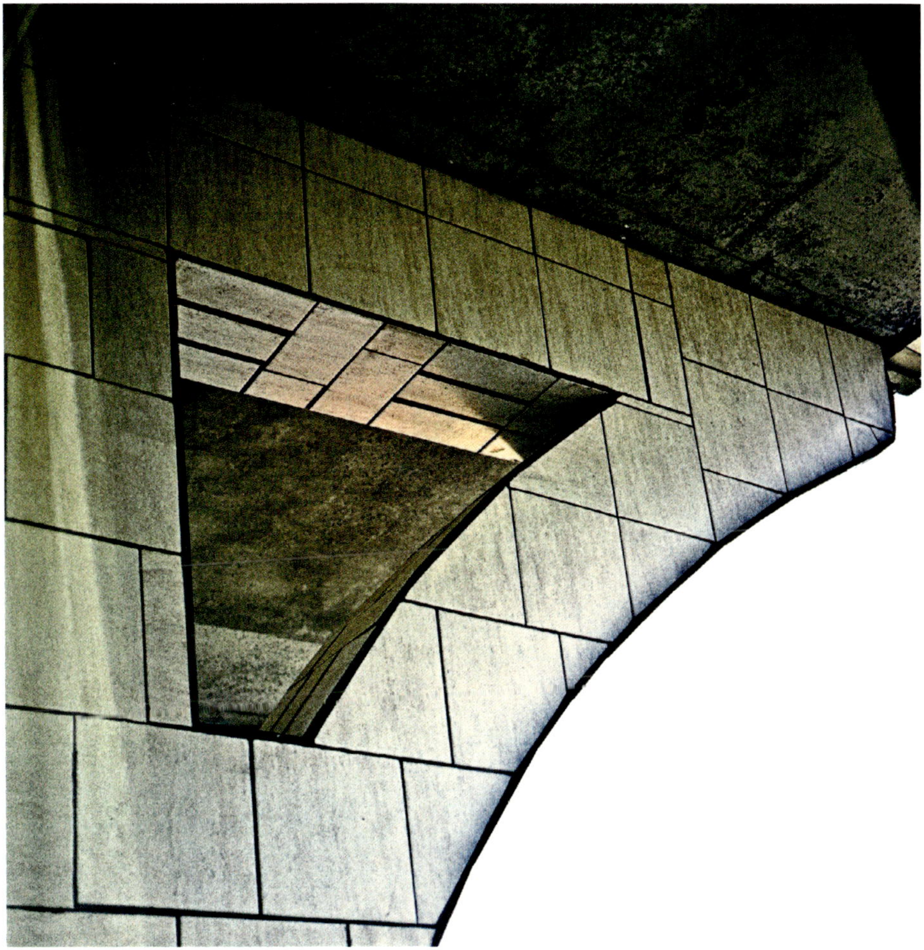

If you set aside your labour costs, how much money did you spend on materials?

Peter: We've been staggered how the money has lasted out. We sold our house in the UK, in Lancaster and when everything was paid for we had, how much?

Linda: Eighty thousand pounds.

Peter: We've still got fifteen thousand of that left, partly because Linda's been working and I have a teacher's pension. The life we lead, apart from the building materials, is quite modest. I used to be, not anxious, but preoccupied about the finances of the project for a long time, five years maybe, and then it became clear that we were going to have enough money to at least get the structure done.

That's very good – but the question I didn't get an answer to was about the Greek State! What kind of interest did you solicit, advertently or inadvertently, from the local government or building inspectors?

Linda: We were once told that you don't need planning permission for a piece of sculpture and we kind of hope that it is seen as a piece of sculpture. It's not just a real estate venture where we're throwing up a building and intending to capitalise on it at some point in the future. That's never been the plan.

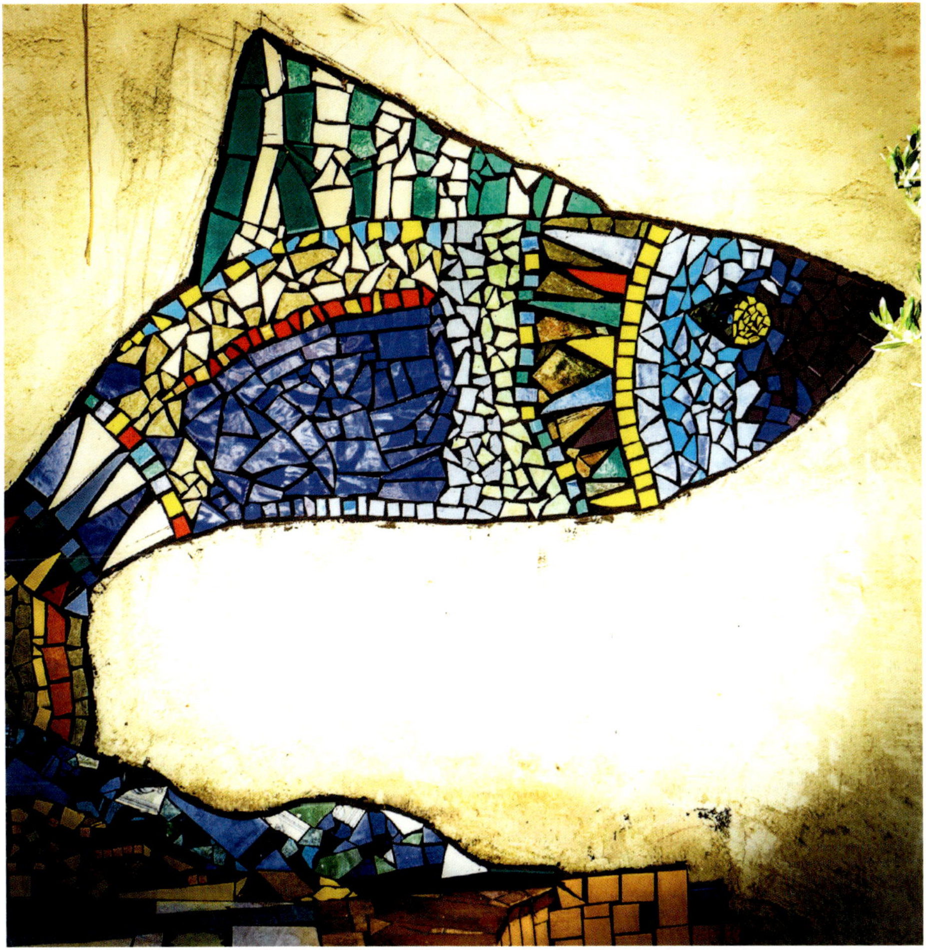

You never get anyone from the government coming to look?

Peter: Oh no, that's not the way Greek bureaucracy works. They want a quiet life, they don't make waves.

That's good.

Peter: The only problem we were told about is that sometimes relations between neighbours in rural areas are not good, so if you have a neighbour who takes agin you, they can sometimes denounce you to the planning office. That happened across the valley actually, so we do know that it happens, though not to us so far. Our relations with our neighbours are, as far as we can tell, uniformly serene.

Linda: They're intrigued by us, I think they're intrigued and they want to know what's going on. They do come and have a look but they quite like it. They do seem to like the fact that it's here.

Peter: Our best advocate is Nikos Avramis, who is an old Greek guy and our neighbour. I've done quite a lot of work for him on his house in the village. I built a kitchen and put timber cladding on some of his concrete ceilings, that kind of thing. So, we always get good press from Niko. There's never been any hint of resentment or antipathy.

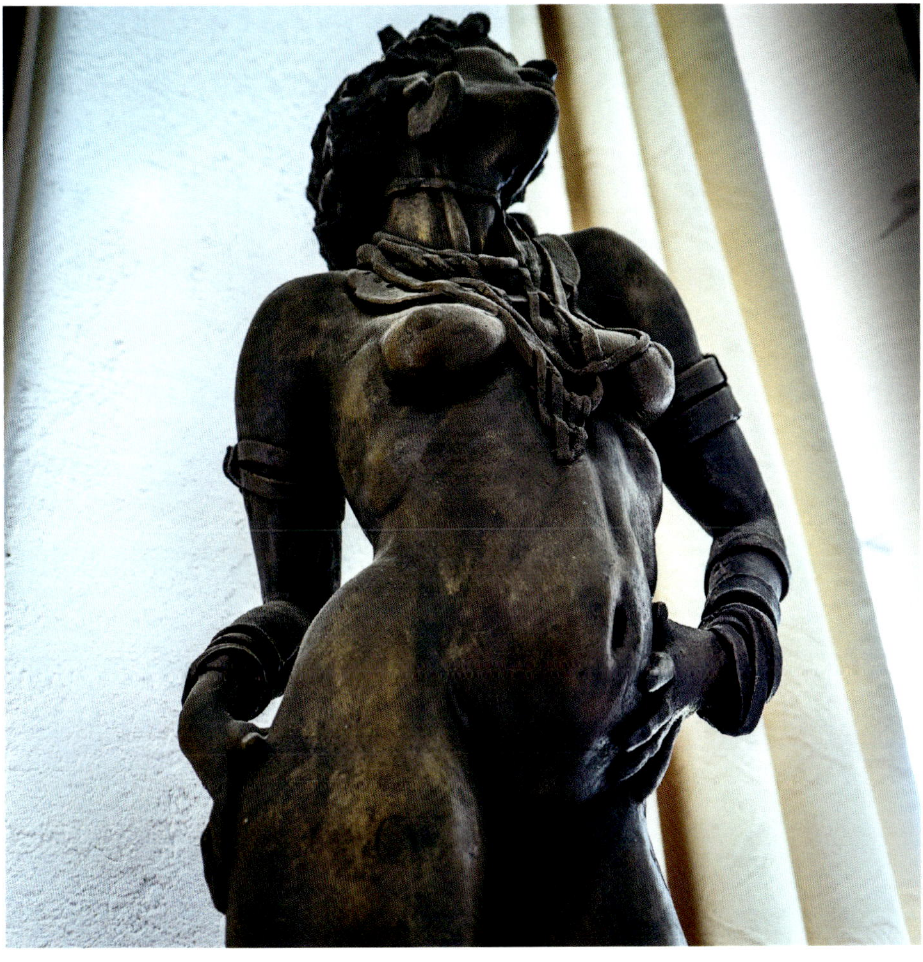

I want to go back to these questions around the cost of different ways of production. When did you have a sense that it was finished? You haven't yet?

Linda: No, not yet.

If you start calling it a 'sculpture' you're going to get into a lot of different sorts of questions that one asks about artworks but which aren't usually asked about buildings, at least not about buildings that are primarily functional. What about the different kinds of 'psychic investment'?

I'm wondering how differently the two of you relate to the erection of the building. Do you have a sense of ownership or authorship that you wouldn't have for a house that you hadn't built yourselves?

Linda: We look at it very differently, I think. It's very definitely Peter's creation, there's no question about that. We do discuss some things and we do come to practical solutions together, but it is his project. Whilst I've done quite a lot of the labour on it, I wouldn't try to claim that I was the 'architect' of the building or anything like that. I do like it, I like it very much and I do feel that we have a good dialogue between us and that it is an expression of both of us, but mostly it's Peter's ideas and also technical skill. He's got a lot of technical skills that I don't have. I've developed some, quite a lot actually, since we started.

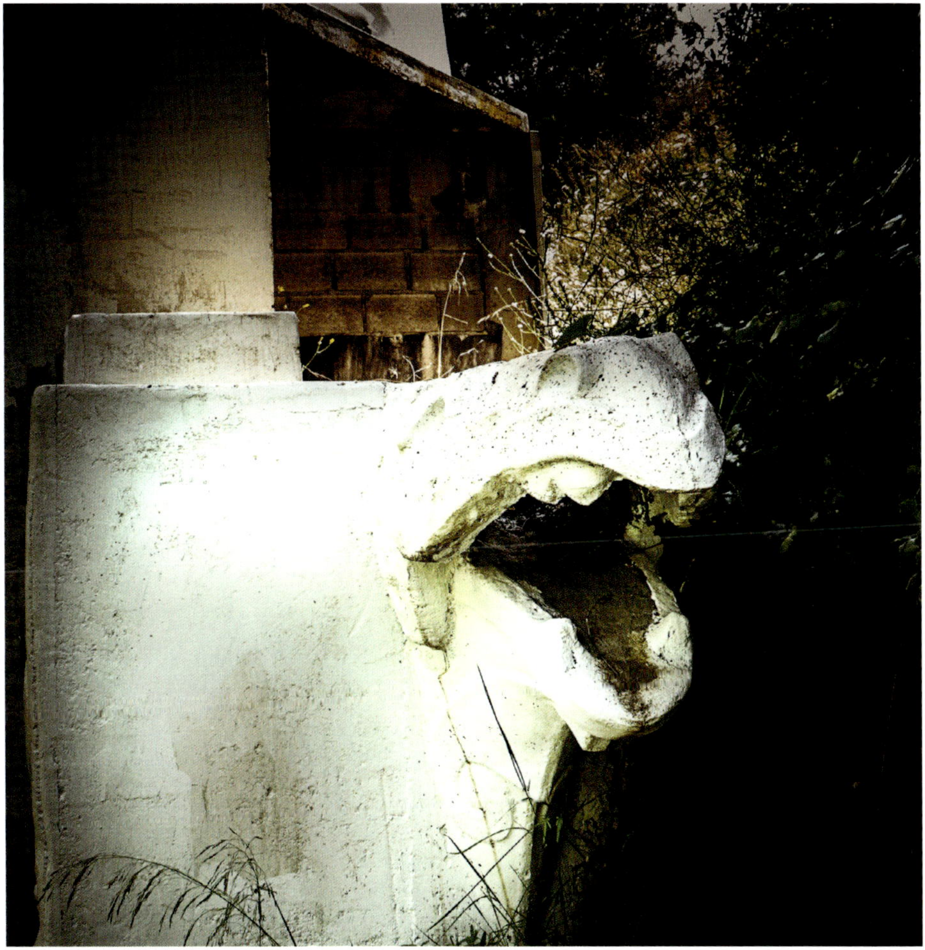

You described the house as a sculpture and this statement raises a big debate in aesthetics about architecture and sculpture – the way the two fields have merged in all sorts of ways and always have done, in some sense. It's definitely a building. It is functional but it has marked symbolic characteristics, doesn't it? Do you think that that's expressed in the way you actually live in it?

Peter: Oh well, leading the aestheticised life has preoccupied us a bit in a jokey kind of way. When you live in a structure like this it does sometimes make you a bit self conscious.

I can see that. The outside looks like a series of very overt walls, you know, pictorial terrains almost, upon which you've created patterns and forms. Is the inside of the building something you thought of as a building rather than as a work of art?

Peter: I'm not sure I think about the project in those terms at all. We get a lot of visitors and you kind of subsist on their responses really. Some of them are more or less blown away by it (laughs.) If it were understood as a monument to pleasure, that would be good enough for me. It does make people smile and it does seem to give them pleasure. That's good enough really, though it's an oblique way of answering your question.

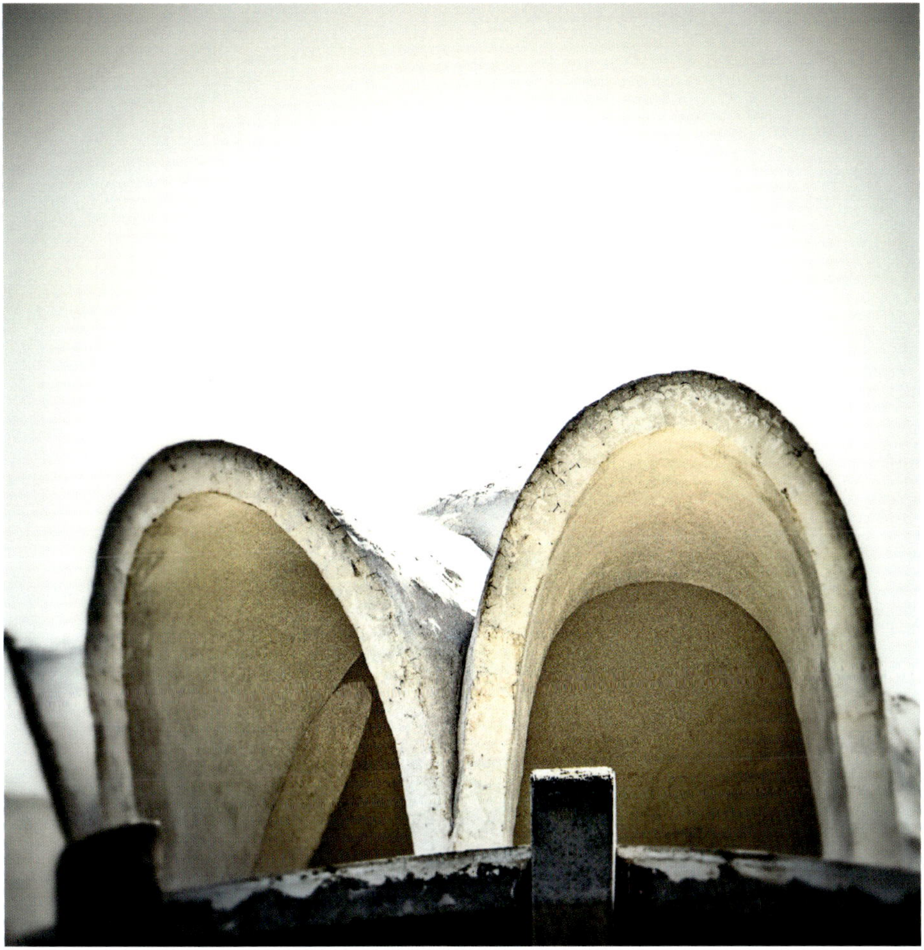

What about the sculptures on the facade of the building, the masks you've done, the heads? What kind of planning, if any, went into the symbolic structure of the façade? How did you decide what to do with a particular wall?

Peter: (laughs) I guess decide is not really in my vocabulary. I just find myself doing it. There is no system. You probably know a book by Geoffrey Scott called The Architecture of Humanism, written in the 1920s. He was one of Bernard Berenson's acolytes. He said our experience of architecture is bodily. The experience of architectural space is to do with the organism, not just the intellect, maybe not even the intellect. What I would say is that I don't make decisions in any conscious way; I just find that that's what I'm beginning to do. There's nothing I could think of as a decision. It's just like a response somehow, I don't know, it's hard to speak about.

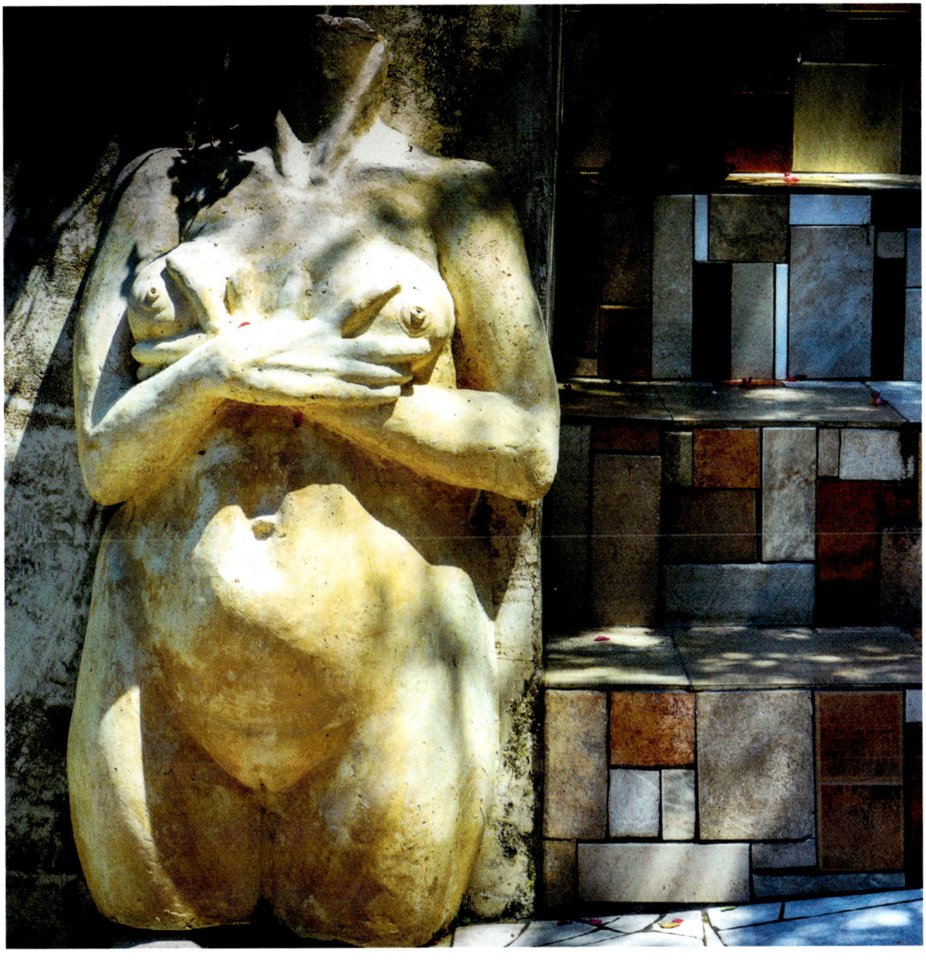

Do you sometimes reflect on the things you've done, about the things that went into the work process and afterwards, in retrospection? Do you find that you are changing your sense, your understanding of it? You live in it, contemplate upon it.

Peter: Yes, but mostly in a practical way. What happens is that the more you do, the more your choices close off. To take the primary example, once you've undertaken to use catenary arches, certain things follow from that, and once big chunks of the structure are there, a lot of the room for manoeuvre is closed off and it becomes obvious what you're going to do next, without bringing it to your conscious mind.

Do you think you actually suppressed thinking about it systematically?

Peter: Yes, absolutely.

How does that work? How is that an active process?

Peter: (laughs) Gosh. Not doing drawings helps. I do sometimes draw bits of sculpture and there are a few drawings hanging about but there's nothing systematic. If you don't draw and if you don't write stuff down, that helps.

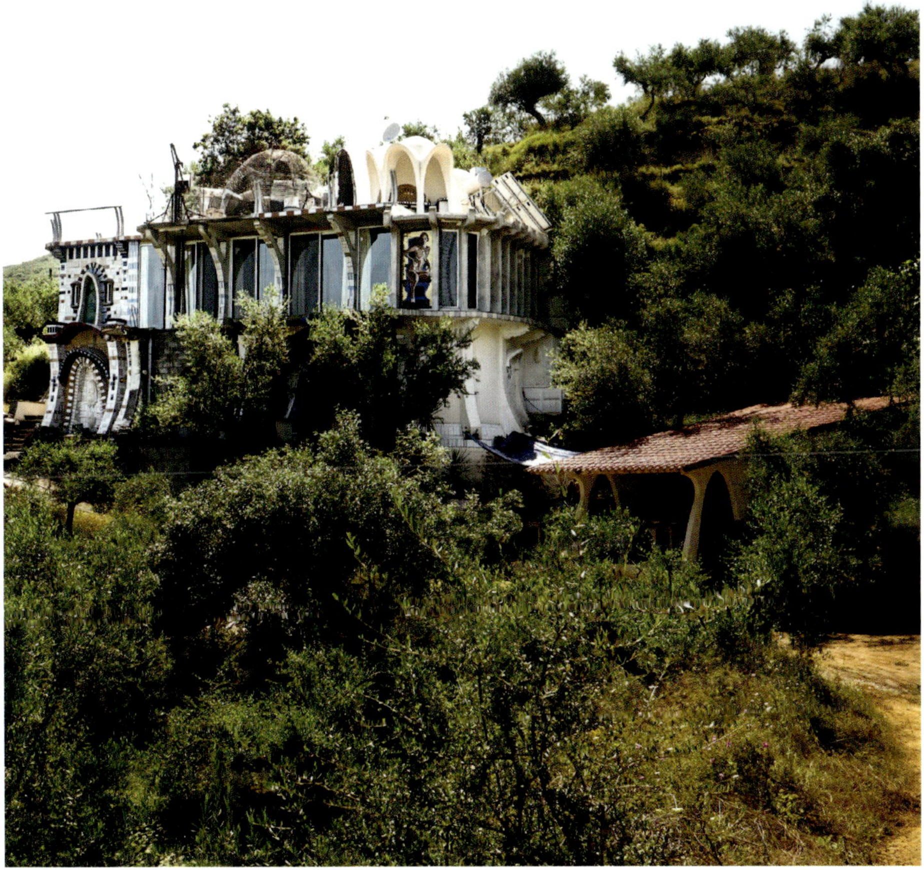

Why have you done that, resisting the idea of thinking it through in a systematic way?

Peter: Well, I hope I'm not going to drift into 'art-bollocks,' but I think that making stuff, for the human species, is utterly fundamental. People make things and it runs very deep in their natures. It's endlessly discussable at one level but in another sense it is not to be spoken about at all. It arises out of some very basic impulses. Speech or any kind of ratiocination is just a commentary on what happens. That's where I want to be really, the space I want to operate in.

But the two things are bound up together, the 'making' and the 'thinking about making', one way or another, aren't they?

Peter: Linda is a dancer and she talks about body memory. You might say that to choreograph a dance requires thought, but the dance itself isn't a 'thinking' thing.

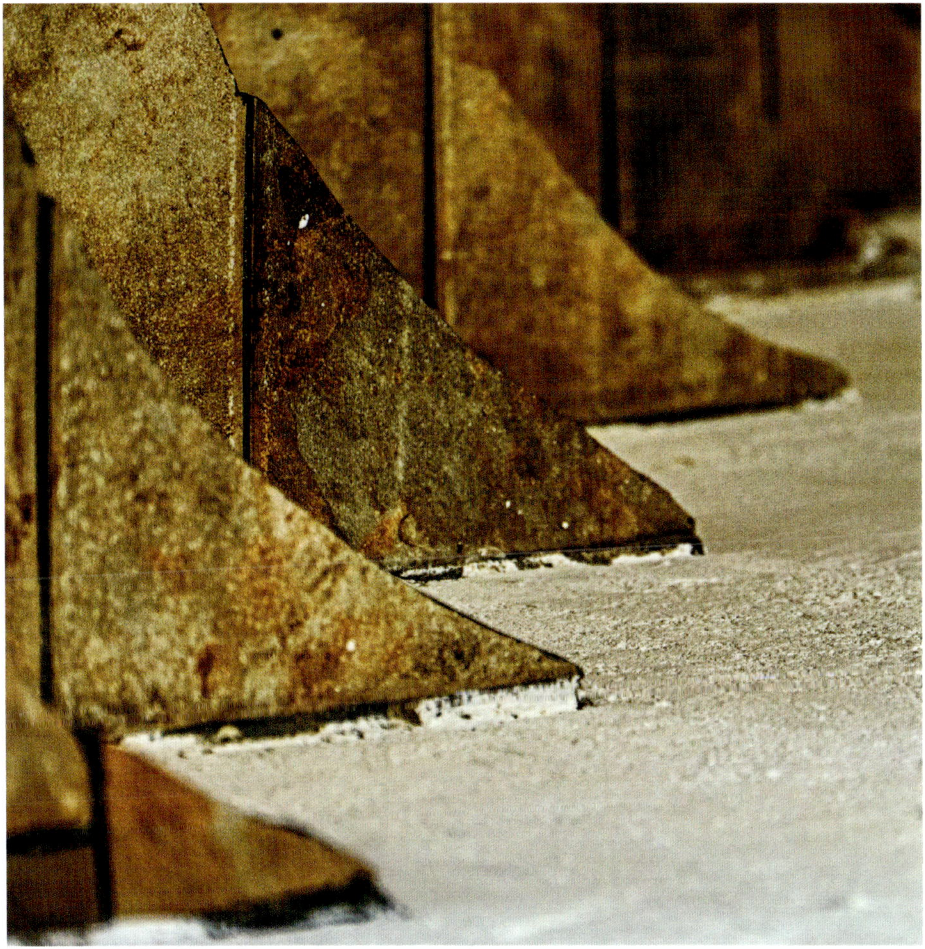

The problem is that thought drives us on to different ways of thinking and doing. We're not thinking of very clear de-facto justifications. It's just the fact that, as humans, we make calculations all the time. That's what interests me about the building. It's bound up with a set of calculations about meanings, as well as materials. This is very clear from its symbolic dimensions and its decorative aspects.

Look at the image of Linda in tile mosaic on the side of the building structure. It has a much more conventional reference to aspects of the history of art, Greek and Roman. I'm just wondering how you manage not to reflect on these things in an organised way. The building is organised.

Peter: In some ways I'm protesting too much, obviously. I'm not a tabula rasa. I know stuff. I know stuff about art history. I have a past, as does Linda, so these things inevitably have some bearing on what you do.

What the building obviously does, in terms of symbolic form, is resist being tied down to any particular frame of reference.

Peter: Bravo, Jonathan. It's very nice when people say that, because a lot of people say 'ah, this house looks like Hundertwasser' or that it's influenced by Antonio Gaudi. It's virtually impossible to make anything that doesn't resonate in some other field. Everything you do reminds you of something else.

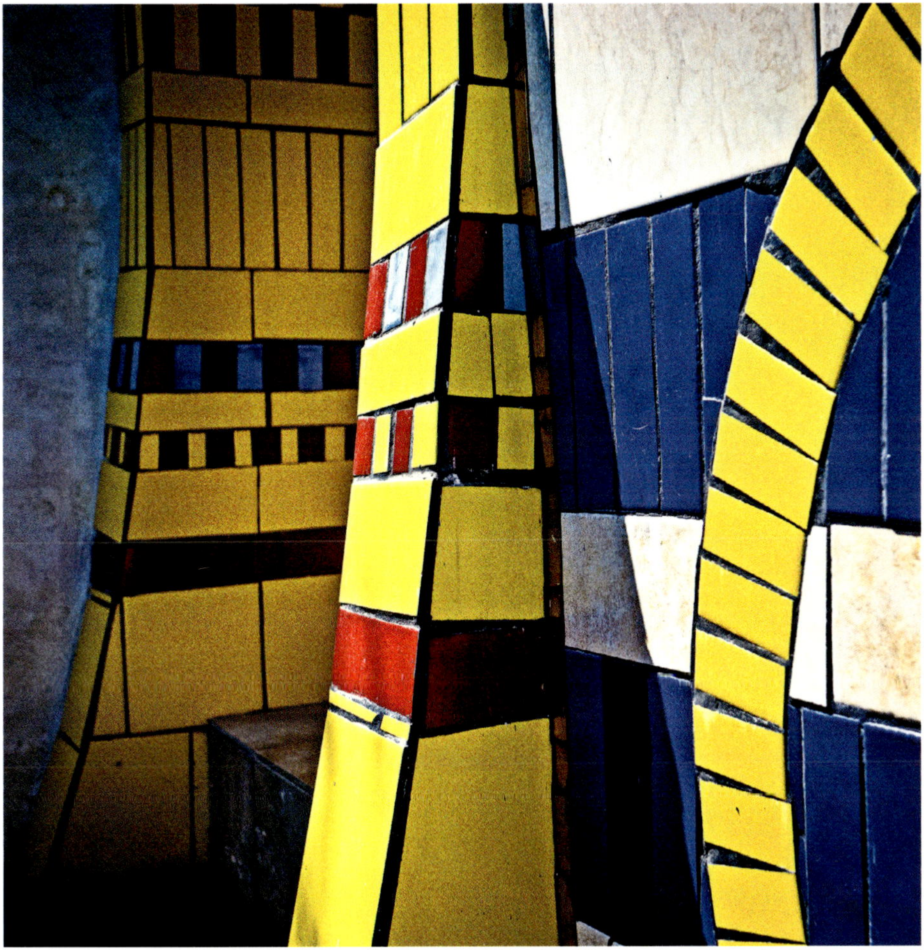

The materials themselves, the tiles – and this is not particularly meant as a criticism – are quite garish, aren't they?

Peter: Yes.

There's an element to it that's a bit like Pop Art.

Linda: Peter is very keen on strong colours. Certainly there was a situation when I was wanting to do browns and more muted colours on some of the catenary arches and Peter said, I don't want any kind of 'good taste' here, so he went for green and red, I think it was.

That's what I was going to say. It definitely avoids good taste.

(laughter)

Peter: Thank you for that.

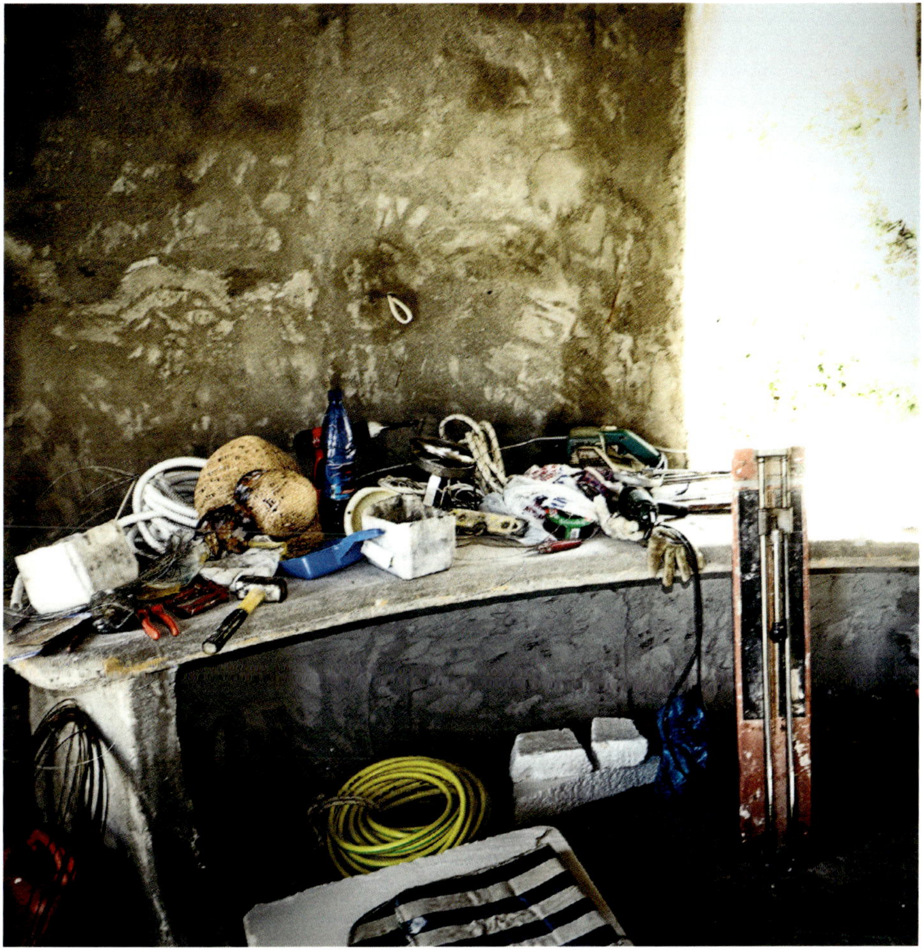

It avoids the conventions of good taste associated with certain kinds of building, anyway. It's not a modernist structure either, is it? It's impossible to tie it down to any particular tradition or frame of reference.

Peter: I hope that's right. The catenary arch, though, has been widely used, the most famous example I guess is the Sagrada Familia in Barcelona. Mathematically it's a very pure concept. It occurs in nature and seems to be a very fundamental phenomenon. A catenary curve, as you probably know, is the curve you get when you suspend a chain or a piece of rope between two fixed points. It can be expressed mathematically.

It reminds me of lot of different things, in 19th and 20th century architecture. There are abstract modernist elements but, also, you get these much more conventional masks, classical and neo-classical references, and you've got this contrast between the garish bright tiles and the images of Linda, the nudes. A bit like something you would see in Pompeii.

Peter: Someone said it looks like a bordello, which made us laugh.

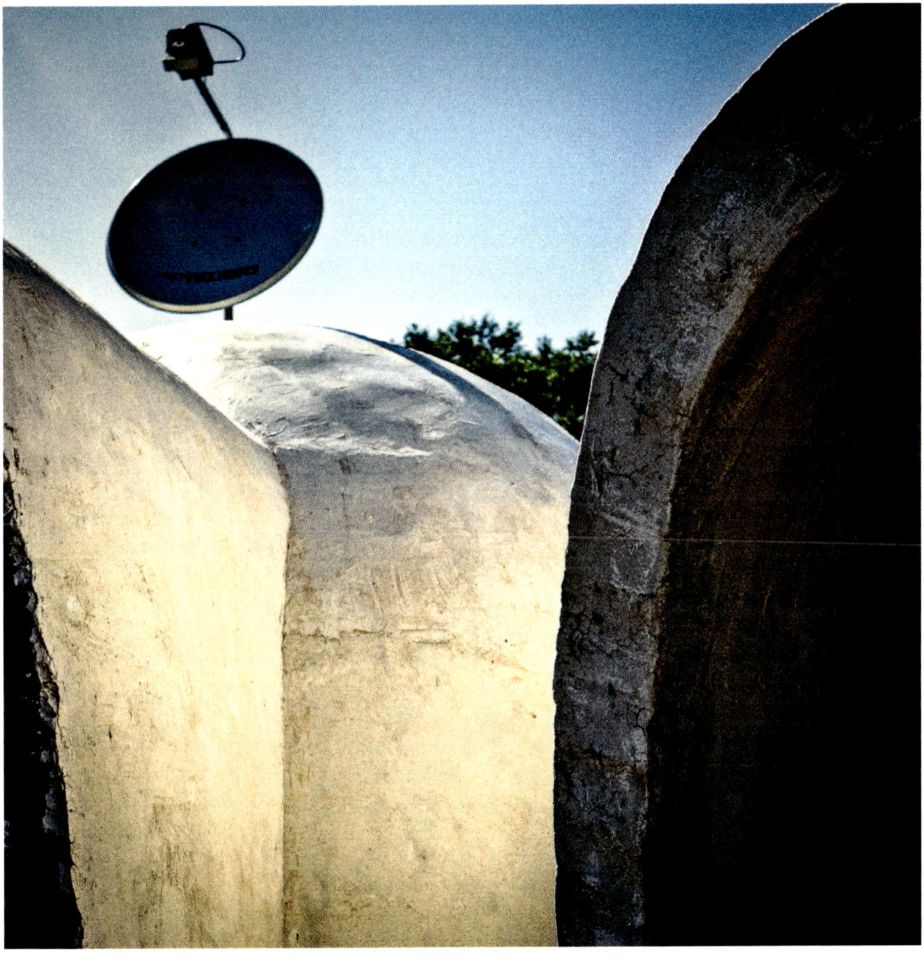

I'm interested now in just talking about how Linda thinks about this, because clearly the building is, in many ways, homage to Linda, as well as to all sorts of other things. What's it like living in this homage to you, Linda?

Linda: It's an interesting question.

Does it make you self-conscious in the morning?

Linda: I don't necessarily see them as images of me. Peter is an artist and we've been together more than twenty years. If he's doing some piece of sculpture that's based on the female form, he'll often use photographs of me as reference material, so, it's not unusual in that sense, but some of these pieces are almost recognisable. They're me and not me, if you see what I mean. It's a massive compliment but it's been going on for so many years now that I don't even think about it anymore really.

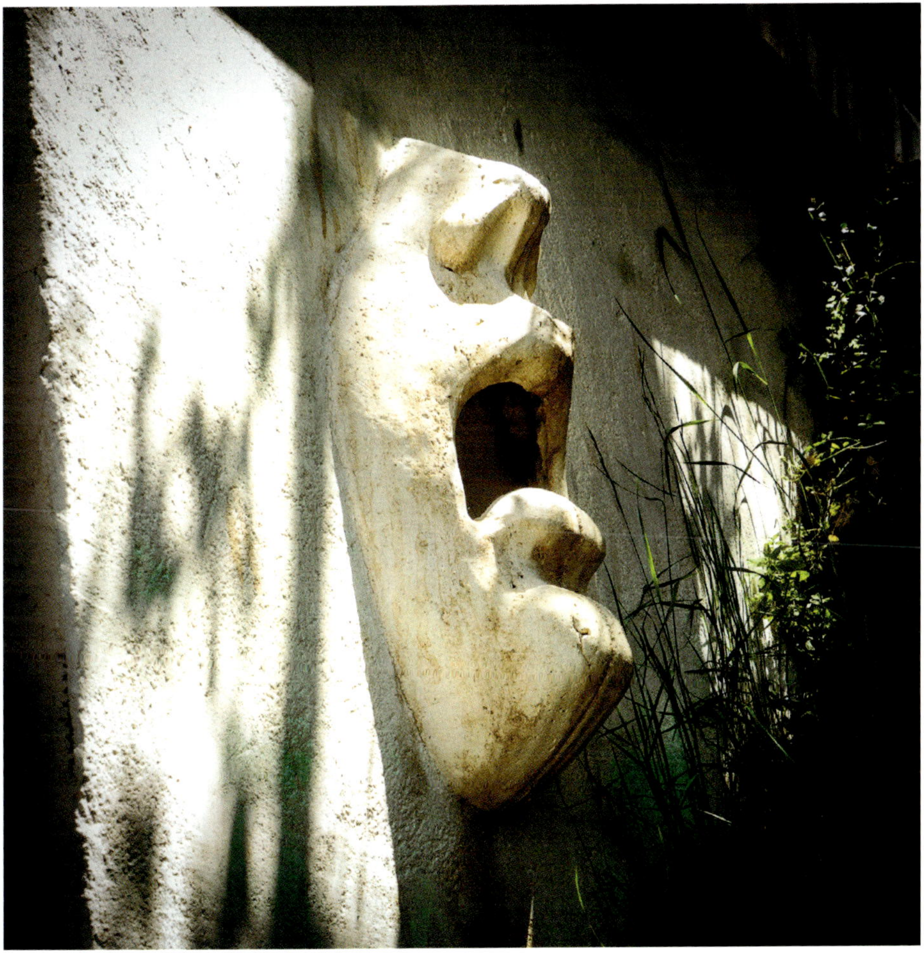

Architects are fond of talking about building forms as 'typologies'. But they're always both generic and specific in their instances. By definition, a house is an actual place that you do have to live in, although it might not conform to certain notions of what a house should be. Now you could say that about all artworks – that in some ways they conform to notions, plans, but then they are material instances with their own specific characteristics in term of site, which is why I think the site aspect here is particularly interesting. It's clear that you have very different senses, correct me if I'm wrong, of 'proprietorial relations' to this place and site. Is that right, Peter, would you say?

Peter: I say I could walk away from this project tomorrow, and I'm sure it's true. I've done it before. I did start a biggish building project years ago which I left for other reasons, exoteric reasons. I don't have an investment in this one. I'm not sentimental about it at all. I enjoy the process really, just the business of doing it.

I didn't mean that you couldn't walk away from it, but that the materials upon which it has been built involve deep internal investments.

Peter: Yes, I like stuff.

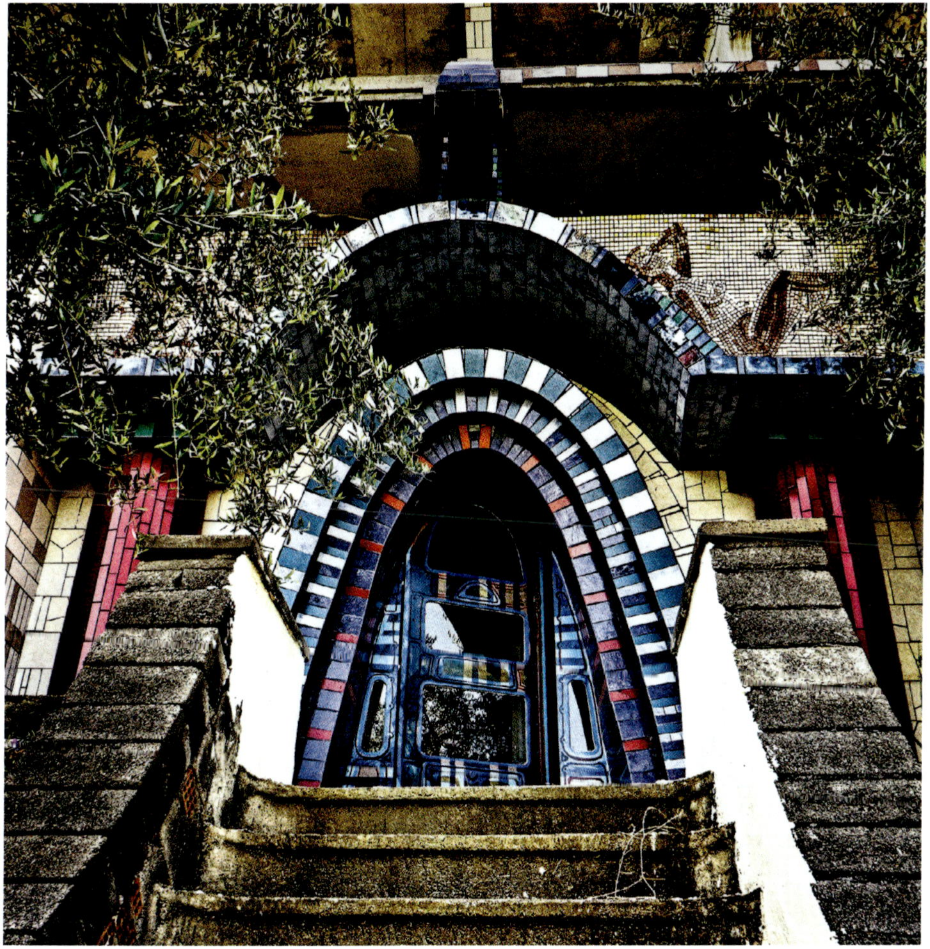

In all sorts of ways: ‘woman’, ‘Linda,’ ‘labour’ – which have their own kind of reward and those are the investments that the building represents, aren’t they?

Peter: Yes I can see that, I think. I don’t want to be in any other space really. It’s an excellent life. I feel very privileged. That sounds like a mawkish thing to say, but I do. My dad was a builder, a labouring man and I had a working class upbringing. I look out over the bay and I just feel a very distinct sense of good fortune.

And yet the actual structure, what you’ve brought to it, and your background, are very different from most of the other people who live in that area, the ‘locals’ as it were. The house has been implanted here from a very wide and diverse exogenous set of circumstances. You’re not trying to conform or fit into a particular kind of convention of building in that area, are you, a Mediterranean-type building?

Linda: No it’s definitely unique in this area I think (laughs).

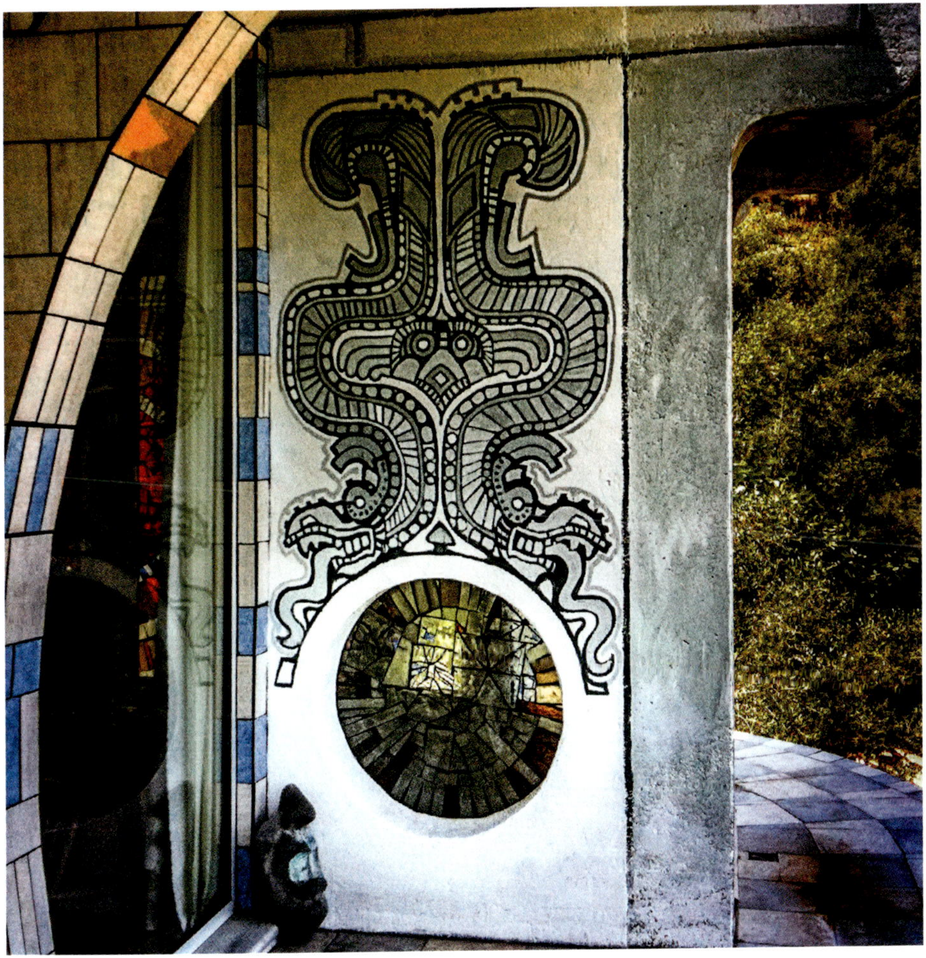

Do you ever get any negative reactions or people who are quite angry about it?

Peter: Never. I guess the mechanism is that if people didn't like it they wouldn't say, but when people walk up to it gives us both great pleasures when they just smile and laugh. It seems to bear them up. We ourselves had a similar experience when we went to Nikki de San Phalle's Tarot Garden complex, north of Rome. Linda and I went there three or four years ago.

You watch people approaching and they just smile. They are just borne up by the pleasure embedded in it. That's good enough. If that's what this building generates in the people who see it then I'm very happy.

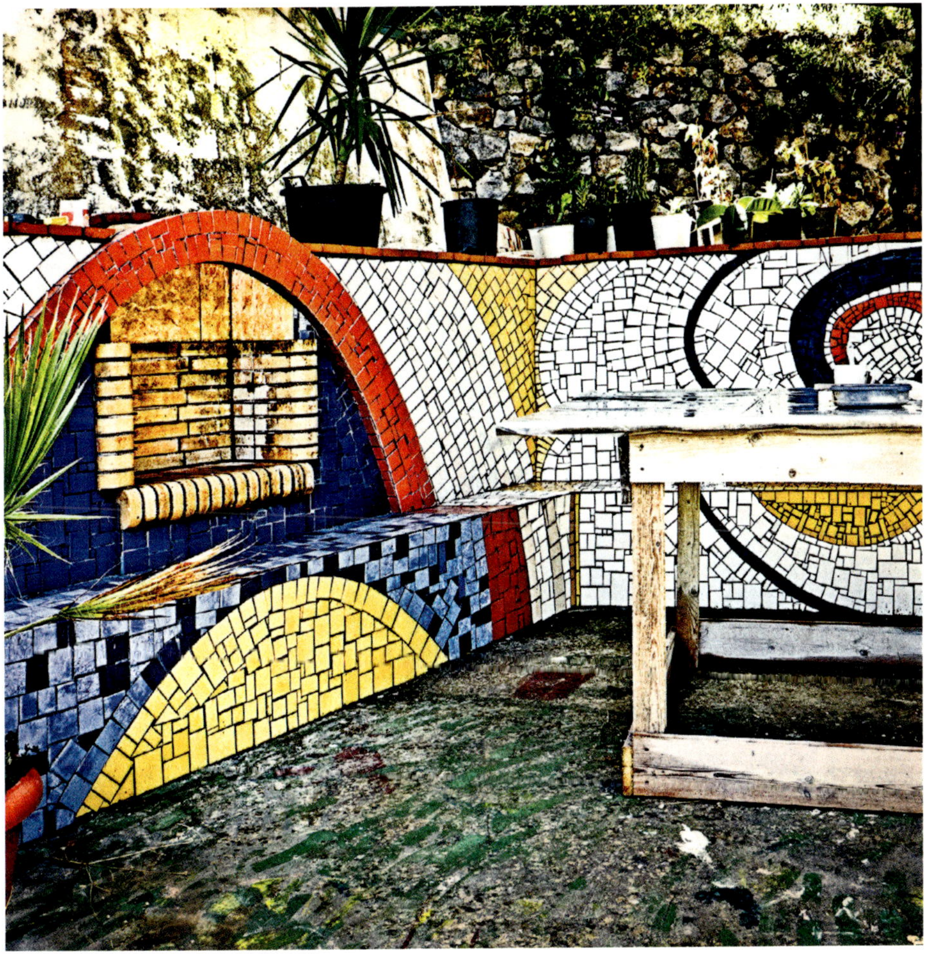

Your house is clearly a Work of Art, isn't it, as well as being a building? The two add up together. Do you think about it as an artwork separately from it being a building? Or do the two codes relate to your understanding of it, would you say?

Peter: Over all my years of doing stuff, I have tried not to identify myself as an artist anyway. It just gets in the way really. You develop a kind of pose if you allow yourself to be characterised as an artist. I model myself, and this is bizarre, on my father. My father did jobs. He was a builder. He would go to some place and do some work and when the work was finished he would go elsewhere and work. That's the world I live in I think. I don't think I'm being dishonest.

Linda: Except that Peter's lucky enough to be able to do the work in the place where he lives so he can keep it and he can build on it. One of the things we say to people who say oh my god there's a lot of work here, is if, like you for example, Jonathan, you could see your work in solid form, if you could pile it all up in one place, it would be enormous. What Peter has here is the privilege of being able to do that and keep it because it's our land.

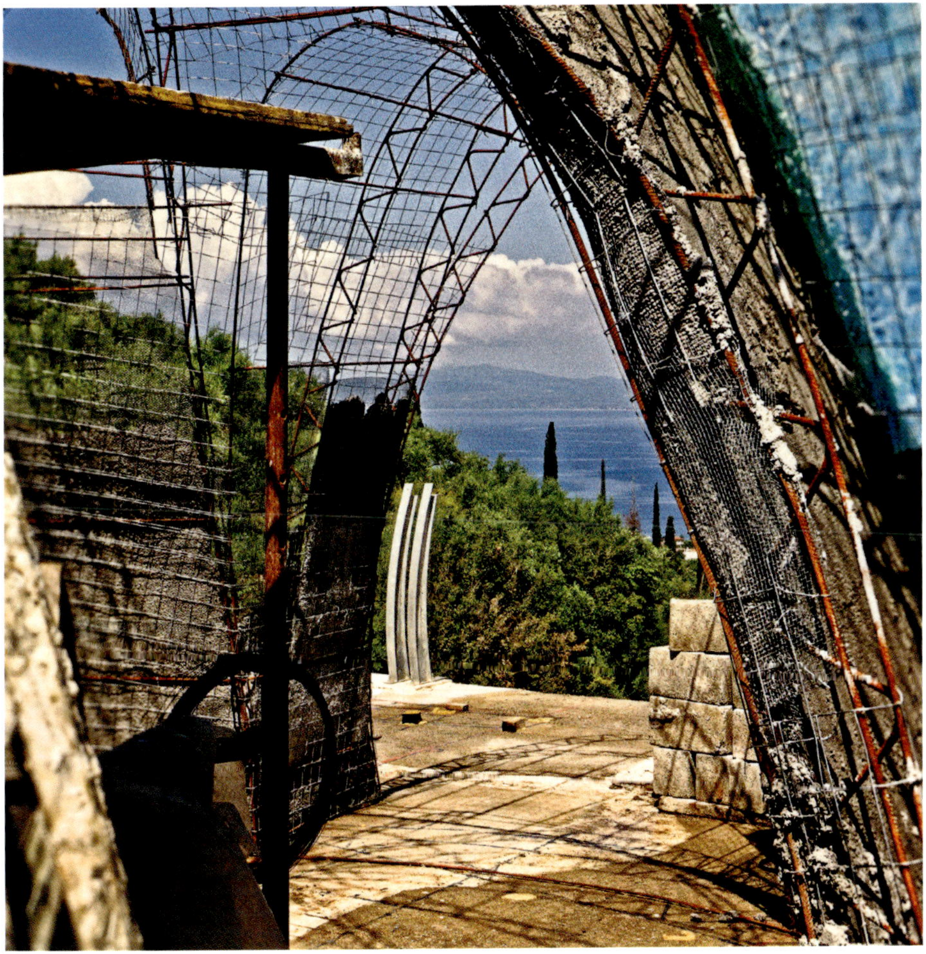

I think there's an interesting question there, in the light of conceptual art, going back to the 1970s, which has really dominated contemporary art for a long time in some ways. There was recognition then that there was already enough art, enough things in the world.

Peter: I agree, yes. (laughs)

If you are building a sculpture which is also where you can live... you can see where I'm going with this... then there's a justification and a raison d'etre for it which goes beyond simply producing another beautiful commodifiable structure.

Peter: I absolutely concur. It takes a weight off your shoulders. A painter, for example, must simply stand in front of his work. People pass judgement on the painting, whereas, if it's a house, you somehow evade that difficulty.

If someone offered to buy it off you, what would you ask?

Peter: I can't imagine who would. (laughs) I don't know the answer. We would sell it probably, though I've no idea what the price might be.

Linda: And move on to something else.

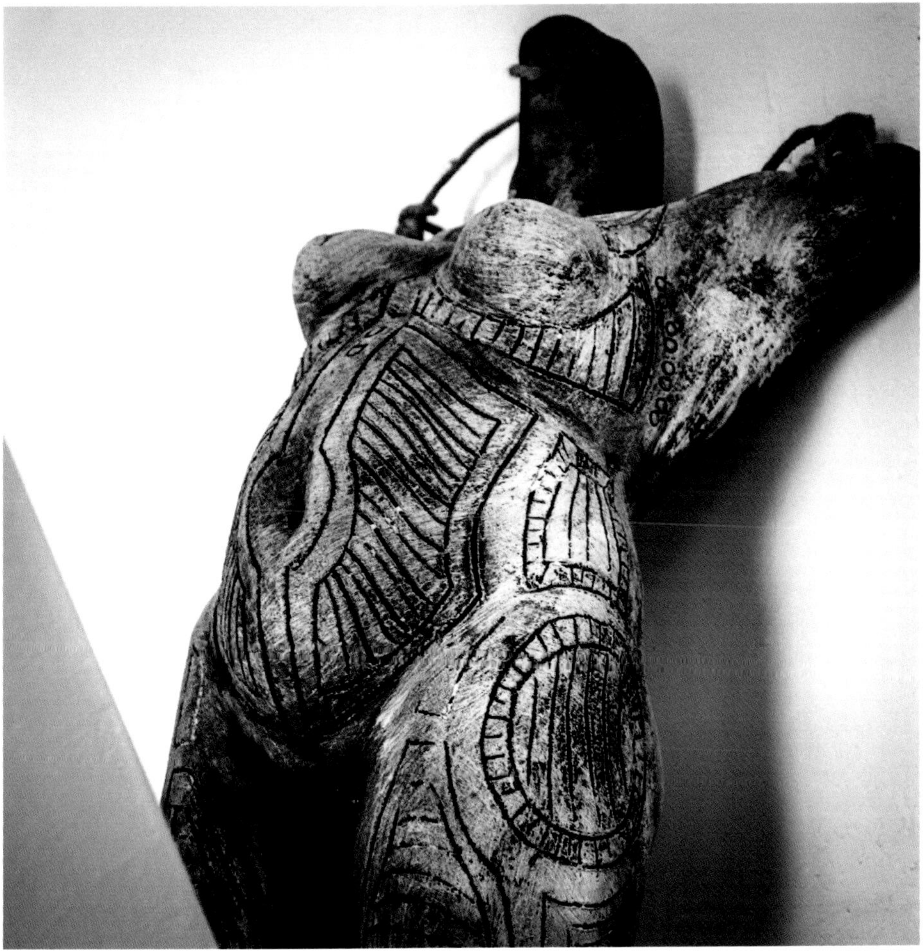

It's intriguing to consider 'alienated labour,' because normally we think about labour done for others, you know, work in that context as being alienated. We tend to have a different notion of work done for ourselves or work done in the family, between parents, for instance, with kids around, housework done by one or other of the two people. But you seem to be saying that your attitude toward this product of your own labour is no different from labour you would have done for someone else on a paid basis. Is that right, Peter?

Peter: Yes, in the sense that it's the 'process' that counts with me. It's being in the process, on the road. That's where I want to be. I don't want particularly to be associated with anything that's finished.

The sculpture, the architecture, perhaps, becomes a kind of residue?

Peter: Absolutely. It's like the ash, what's left behind.

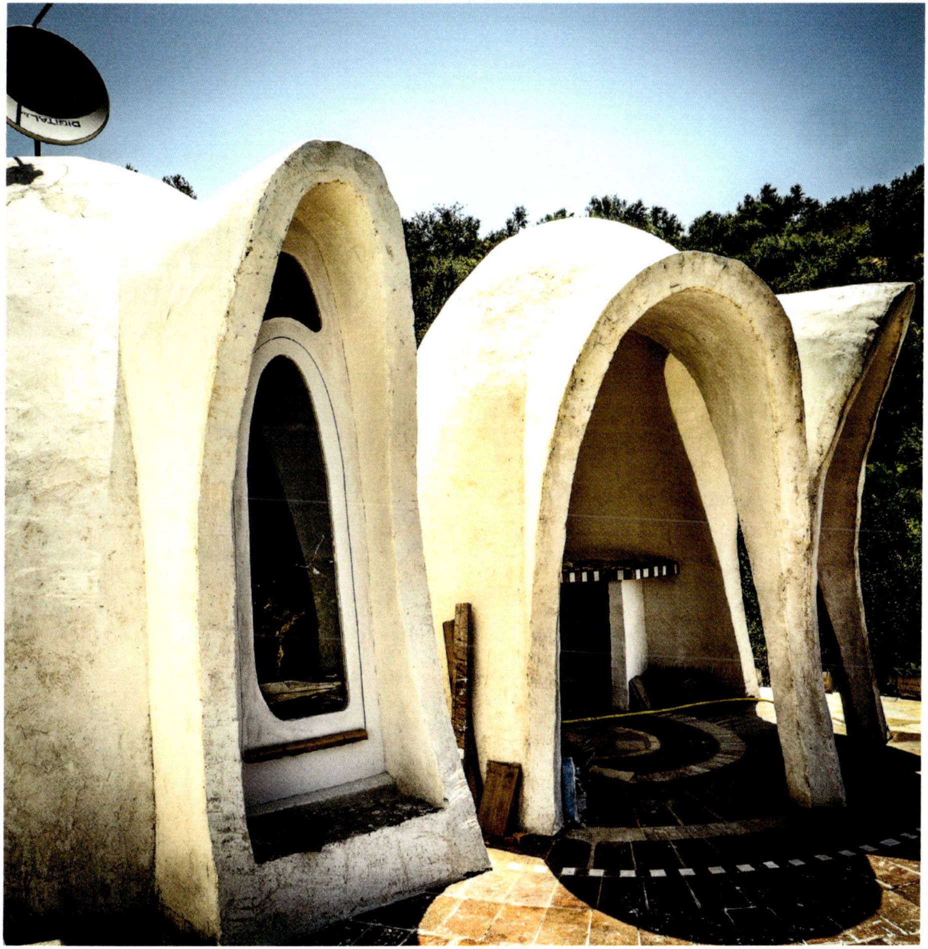

In some ways I feel the same way about my own writing. Once I've done it I don't really care much about it anymore. I can't stand dealing with publishers because they obviously go over everything that you did years ago. But the difference is that you are living in this house. I can't live in my books!

(laughter)

Peter: You could pile them up...

Do you think you might come to resent the house at some stage?

Peter: Yes. It has happened with other work I've done before, actually. If I work in a place for long enough it becomes like a museum. It's happened to me twice in the past, but I'm now somewhat older than I was.

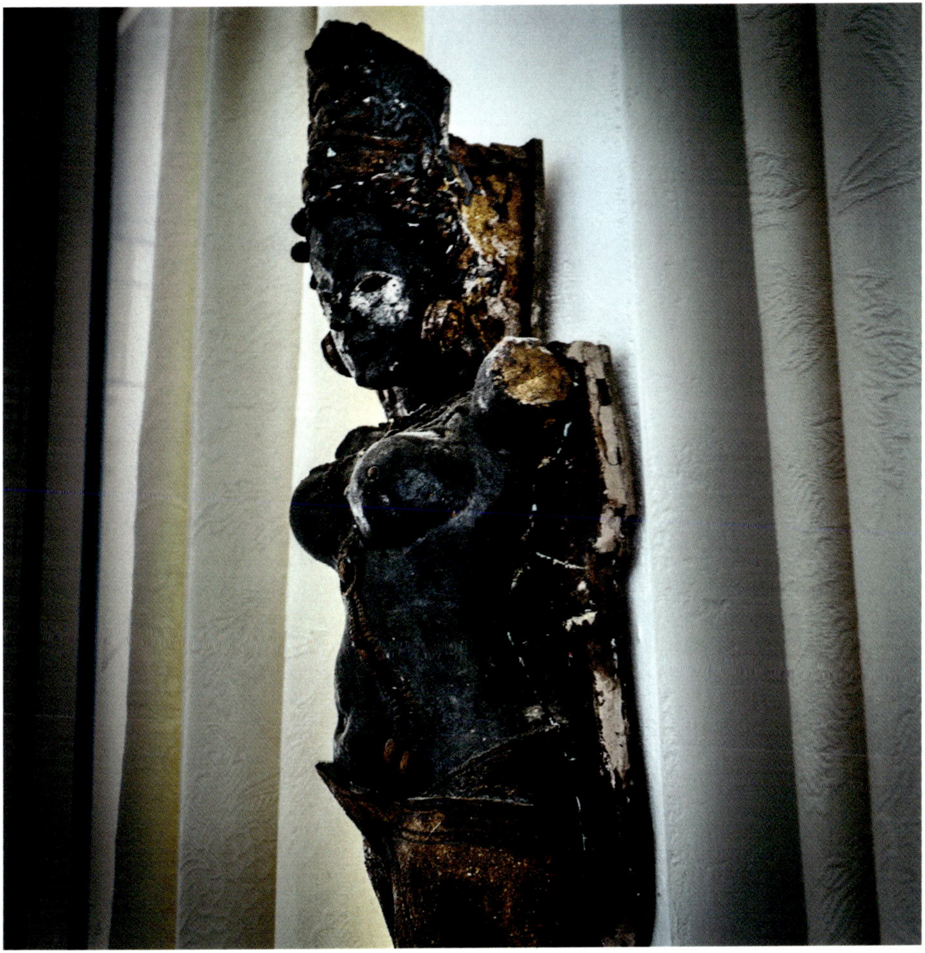

What more things do you have to do to the house? How do you carry on keeping it a living, developing project, rather than dead residue?

Peter: What I really came here to do was to make big pieces of sculpture, actual sculpture. I used to do sculpture in the UK and you couldn't do anything big unless you had somewhere to put it and now I've got a lot of space to put stuff, out there in the olive groves. In fact, I'm about to start on a big, twice life-sized figure that sits by the roadside. Probably the whole site will be full of my debris, depends how long I'm spared I suppose. (laughs) If I last another ten years, there'll be a lot more stuff.

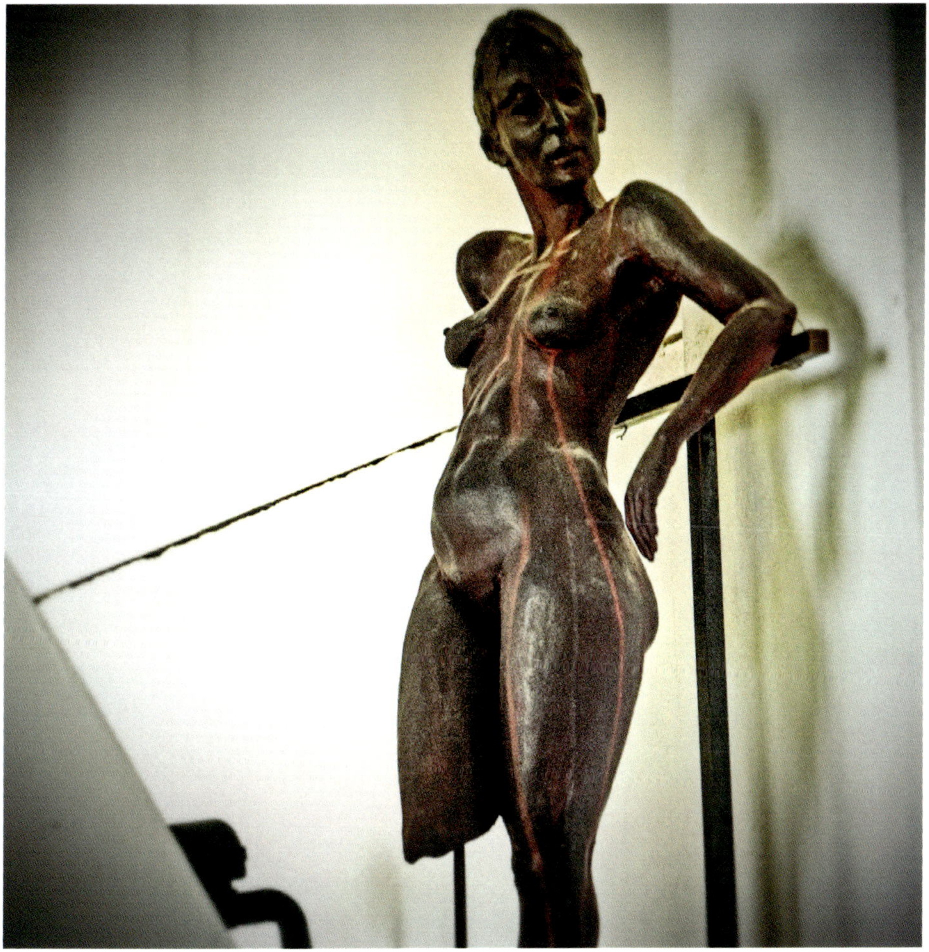

What about you, Linda? How do you feel about this, because in some ways what Peter is saying about the house constitutes an acknowledgement of ambivalence to both production and meaning? Its 'living thing' while the structure is in the process of creation, but when it's finished it becomes something else, it may congeal into something less.

Linda: Yes, well again, I've lived with him for a long time, and I know that he likes what he's doing until he has finished it, a bit like you, maybe. I don't know whether you're still pleased with your books when you've finished them, but usually, when he's finished, he doesn't even want to look at it for a long time. What do I feel? It's a nice place to be and I enjoy being here. We've been seven years gradually getting it a bit more comfortable, and now we're quite comfortable. It's quite nice, an easy place to be, and it's always good to meet people when they come here and see it and they enjoy it, and it's nice to have space, but, like Peter, I can imagine us moving on at some point in the future.

It's a very restless attitude.

Linda: Something like that, I don't know. You never know what's in the future, do you.

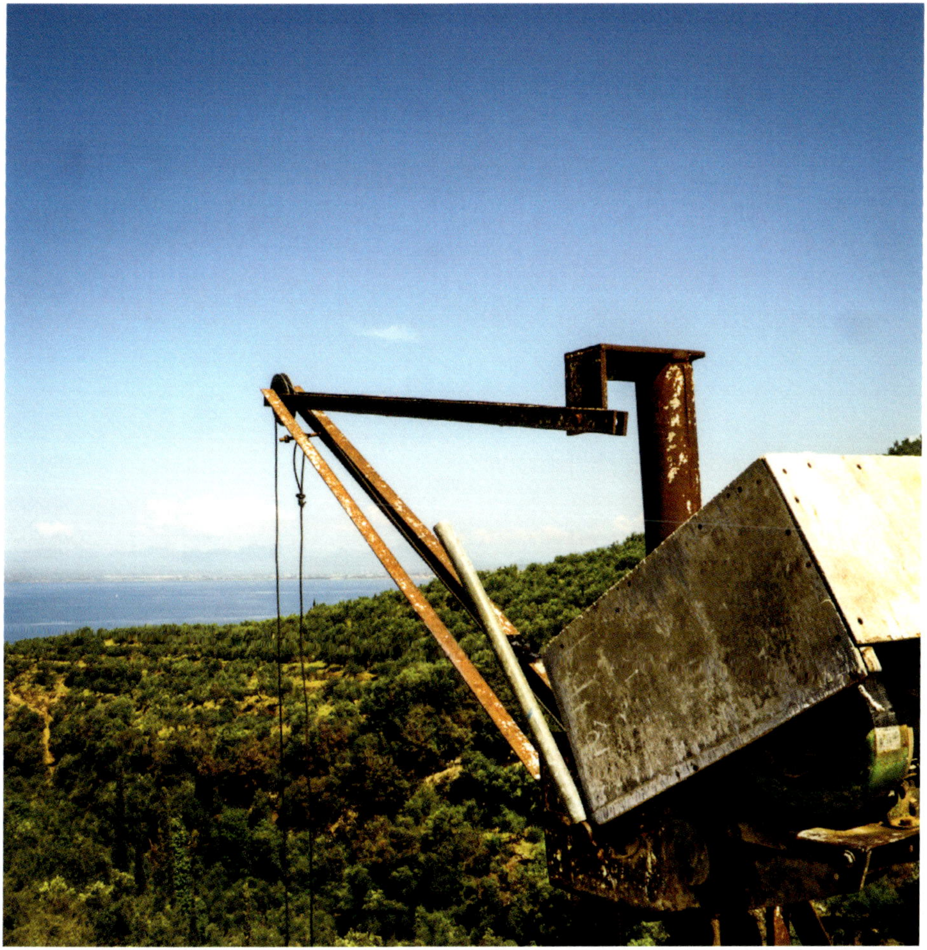

I was going to say – considering you've been in the area quite a long time now – that given what's happened in Greece since 2008, how has your sense of the place, and your place in this place, changed over those eight years?

Linda: A lot. We've got Greek friends...are we talking about the Greek economy?

The social crisis, basically.

Linda: There are definite issues around that. We had some friends here last night, Greeks, and we were talking about the difficulties for them. They're teachers and they're not getting paid. I know I'm a more anxious person than Peter but I worry that if the situation gets much worse and people are literally going hungry, what might happen.

Peter: It seems mostly to be an urban issue. Athens, Patras, Thessaloniki.....that's where the crisis is most painfully felt. Out in the country areas people have less, but Greece is only a generation away from an agrarian economy. In the villages people know how to produce their own food, make their own soap, all that kind of subsistence stuff. In some ways rural Greece is well placed to survive this kind of crisis. Not so in Athens. Athens is very vulnerable. I do think the deprivation there is palpable. The Greeks are very pessimistic at the moment, and they have reason to be. Who knows how the situation will evolve. Watch this space.

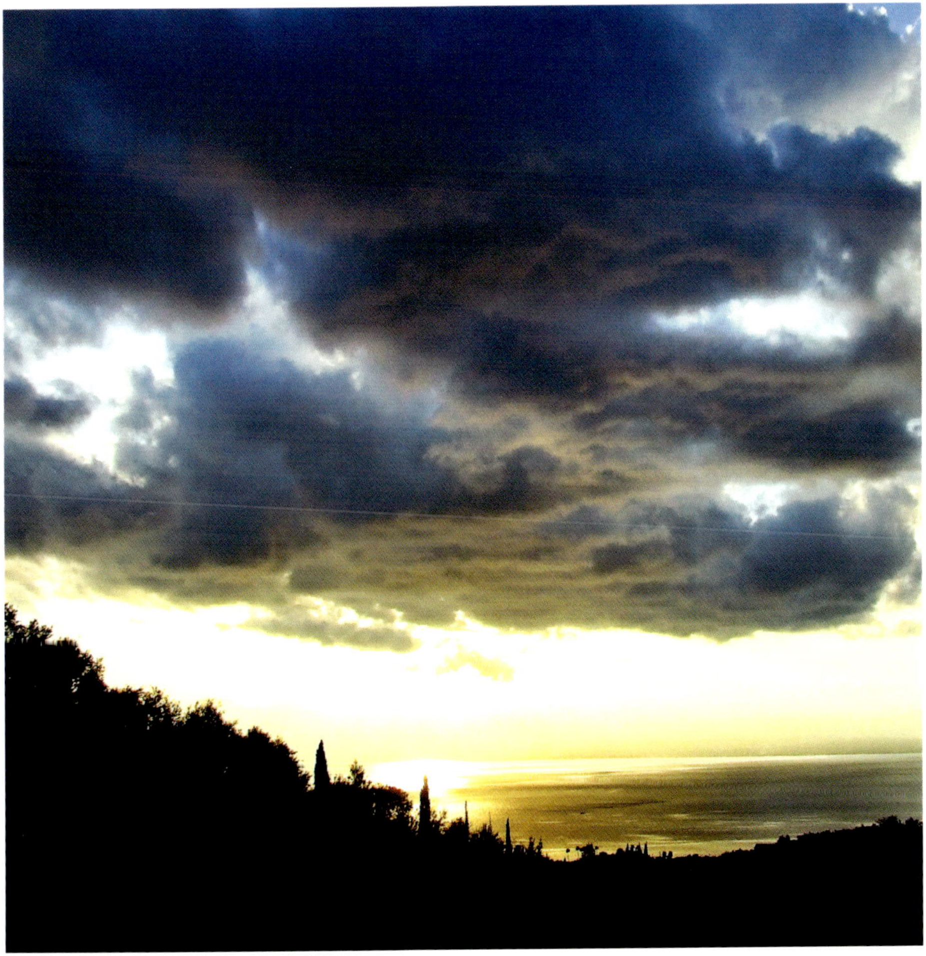

When I came to see it, I immediately realised it was a Peter Huby structure. (laughter) You transport it to wherever you happen to be, the same obsession, concern and deliberation, the obsessiveness of labour that exists everywhere else in your work. In that sense it's a private, internal thing.

Peter: I would agree, I think.

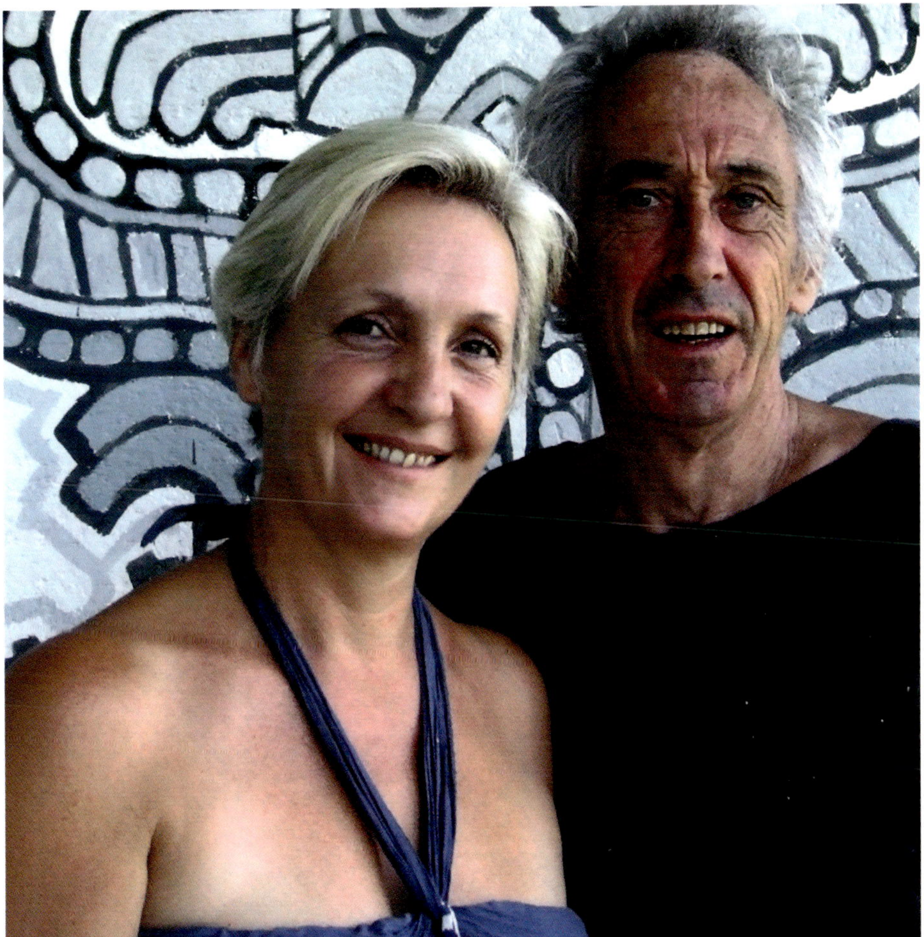

Design by Joseph Joyner

ISBN 978-0-9575182-2-3